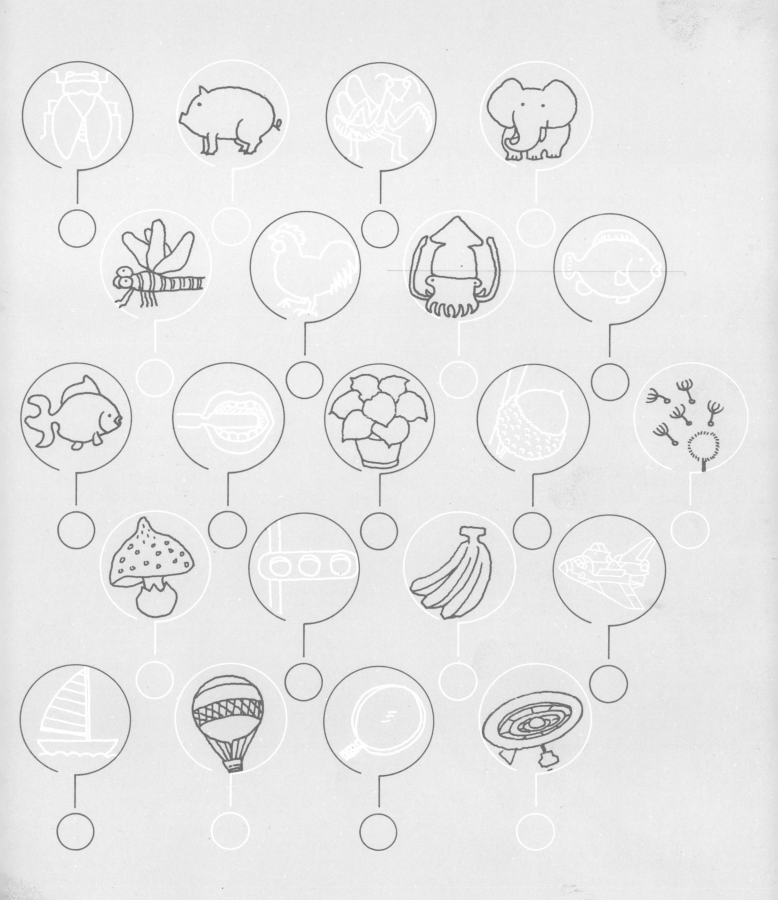

A Child's First Library of Learning

Famous Places

TIME-LIFE BOOKS • AMSTERDAM

Contents

❓ Why Are There So Many Famous Places?

ANSWER Our planet is a very big place. If you could travel round the world, you would discover many wonderful things. You would see beautiful scenery and amazing buildings and monuments. Many are so interesting that they are famous all over the world.

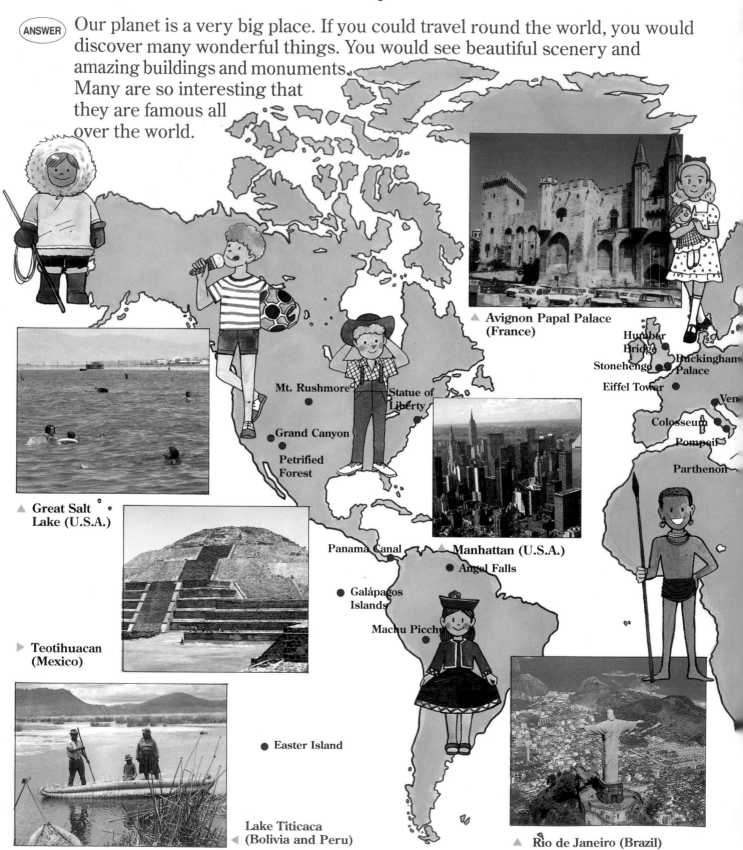

▲ Avignon Papal Palace (France)

Humber Bridge
Stonehenge
Buckingham Palace
Eiffel Tower
Ven
Colosseum
Pompeii
Parthenon

Mt. Rushmore
Statue of Liberty
Grand Canyon
Petrified Forest

▲ Great Salt Lake (U.S.A.)

▶ Teotihuacan (Mexico)

Panama Canal   ▲ Manhattan (U.S.A.)
Angel Falls
● Galápagos Islands
Machu Picchu

● Easter Island

Lake Titicaca (Bolivia and Peru) ◀

▲ Rio de Janeiro (Brazil)

4

Waterloo
(Belgium)

Petrodvorets Palace
(U.S.S.R.)

Lake Baikal
(U.S.S.R.)

Kremlin

▲ Forbidden City (China)

Great
Wall of
China

Seikan Tunnel

Mohenjo-Daro
(Pakistan)

Pyramids

Taj Mahal

Guilin

◀ Hong Kong Island

Aswan Dam

Mt. Kenya
(Kenya)

Great
Barrier Reef

Ayers Rock

▲ Borobudur Temple
(Indonesia)

Olga Mountains
(Australia) ▶

Why Do Soldiers Stand on Guard Outside Buckingham Palace?

ANSWER Buckingham Palace is the London home of the British Royal Family. The soldiers who stand on guard there have the job of protecting this important place from every danger. During the summer months a ceremony known as the Changing of the Guard takes place outside the palace every day at 11:30 a.m. Tourists from all over the world come to see this colourful ceremony, during which new guards replace the ones on duty.

UNITED KINGDOM

London

▶ **The palace guards**

Their red jackets and black bearskin helmets are famous sights.

▼ Buckingham Palace got its name from Lord Sheffield, one of the Dukes of Buckingham. Lord Sheffield had the palace built in 1703.

What Does the Flag Over Buckingham Palace Mean?

Sometimes a flag called the royal standard is seen flying over Buckingham Palace. When it is flying over the palace it means that Her Majesty the Queen is in residence. This is just a formal way of letting people know that the Queen is at home on that day.

? What Are Some of the Other Famous Places in London?

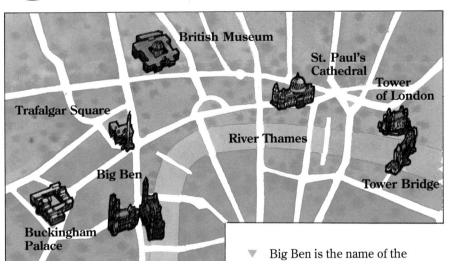

London is the capital of the United Kingdom. Many of its old buildings are important for historical or cultural reasons. The map shows where some of the famous ones are.

▼ **Tower Bridge.** The middle of this bridge can be raised to allow big ships to pass under it and continue on their way up or down the River Thames.

▼ Big Ben is the name of the bell in the clock tower of the Houses of Parliament.

● **To the Parent**

The Changing of the Guard is one of London's famous sights. Crowds of tourists gather to watch the guards marching in perfect time. These soldiers guard the palace, which is the London home of Britain's ruler. Queen Victoria was the first monarch to live here. A monument to her stands in front of the gate. The British Empire was at its peak during her reign, and this monument has become a symbol of Britain's imperial glory.

❓ What Is It About This Bridge That Makes It So Famous?

ANSWER

This is the Humber Bridge, in northeast England. It is the longest suspension bridge in the world. The bridge measures 1,410 metres from one main support to the other. If all the wire used in the cables were laid in a straight line it would measure about 70,800 kilometres, or almost enough to go around the entire earth twice.

◀ The Humber Bridge is used by both cars and pedestrians.

UNITED KINGDOM

Humber Bridge

London

■ How a suspension bridge is measured

The distance between the two main supports is the bridge's span.

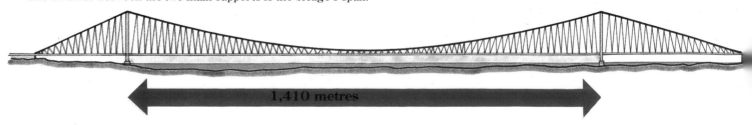

1,410 metres

Different Types of Bridges

There are many types of bridges. When building a bridge, people have to think about such things as strong winds and what materials to use. And they must know what traffic will pass over it, and under it too.

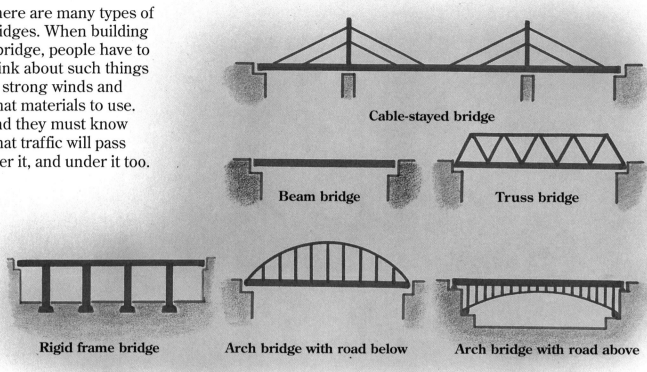

Cable-stayed bridge

Beam bridge

Truss bridge

Rigid frame bridge

Arch bridge with road below

Arch bridge with road above

Three unusual types of bridges

■ **Drawbridge.** The middle opens and rises so that ships can pass beneath it.

■ **Vertical lift bridge**

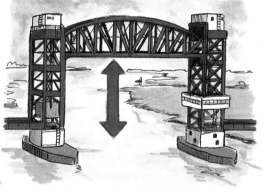

The whole bridge is raised to let large ships pass under it.

■ **Swing bridge.** It swings to the side to let big ships through.

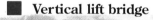

● **To the Parent**

The suspension design is most suitable for bridges with very long spans. All of the world's big long-span bridges, including the Humber and the Golden Gate Bridge in California, are of this type. These bridges hang from cables strung between two towers. The longer the span, the higher the towers must be.

The Stonehenge Mystery: What Were These Huge Stones For?

ANSWER This giant stone circle in southwest England is about 3,500 years old. The stones are from five to nine metres high and weigh between 25 and 45 tonnes. We know that Stonehenge was built by ancient people, but why they built it is a mystery. Some people think that the stones may have been placed to form a sort of calendar.

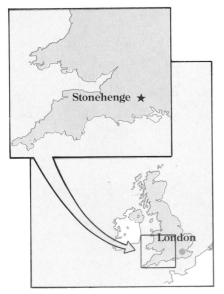

One way that Stonehenge might have

First a trench was dug in the earth. One of its sides sloped at an angle. Then one of the big stones was slid into it.

Next, the stone was lifted using logs, as shown on the left. Then the job was completed with ropes, as in the picture above.

Was Stonehenge Used to Study the Sky?

Scientists have used computers to show that the stones may have been put in positions to mark the changes of season.

First, a large circular trench was dug. Earth was piled up on both sides of this trench.

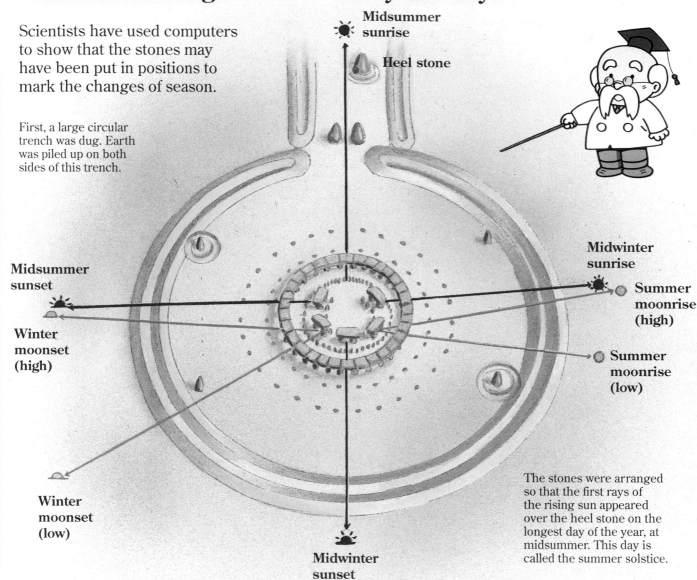

Midsummer sunrise

Heel stone

Midwinter sunrise

Summer moonrise (high)

Summer moonrise (low)

Midsummer sunset

Winter moonset (high)

Winter moonset (low)

Midwinter sunset

The stones were arranged so that the first rays of the rising sun appeared over the heel stone on the longest day of the year, at midsummer. This day is called the summer solstice.

been built

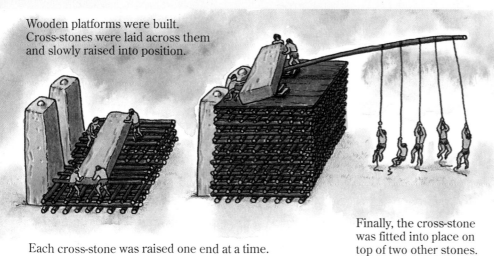

Wooden platforms were built. Cross-stones were laid across them and slowly raised into position.

Each cross-stone was raised one end at a time.

Finally, the cross-stone was fitted into place on top of two other stones.

● **To the Parent**

The original layout, shown in the drawing above, consisted of an outer ditch and bank about 105 metres across. Inside this were three rings, one of 60 holes and two of 30 holes each. Inside these was a circle of stones, 30 metres in diameter. Inside that was a circle of much smaller stones and holes and a U-shaped arrangement of stones up to nine metres high surrounding an altar stone. It seems possible that it was used as a place of worship by an ancient people, but the sort of worship that may have been involved is not really clear.

Why Was This Tower Built?

ANSWER In 1889, a great public exhibition was held in Paris. This tall tower was built especially for the exhibition. It was named after the man who built it, Alexandre-Gustave Eiffel. People were amazed because nothing like it had ever been built before. Today, the Eiffel Tower is famous all over the world. Every year millions of tourists go up to a platform at the top to enjoy a wonderful view of Paris.

▼ **Eiffel Tower**

When it was first built the Eiffel Tower was only 300 metres high. But now radio and TV transmitting antennae have been added, bringing it up to 321 metres. Surprisingly, the tower took just 17 months to build.

● **To the Parent**

When people think of Paris today they invariably think of the Eiffel Tower. It is considered the very symbol of Paris. But when the tower was built in 1889 it was widely criticized. Many people felt that it was too modern for the traditional skyline of Paris.

Where Are Some of the World's Tallest Structures?

New building methods and materials enable people to build taller and taller structures.

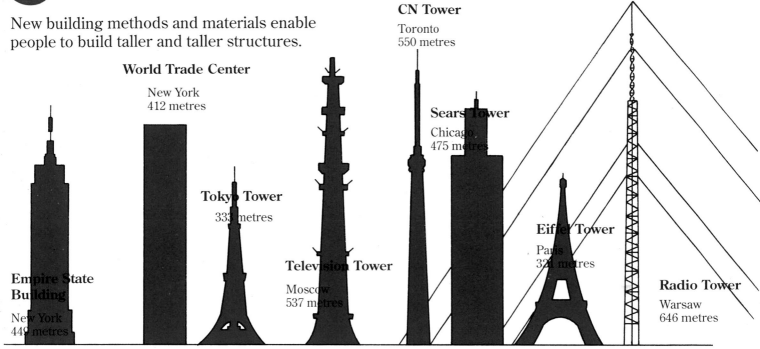

CN Tower
Toronto
550 metres

World Trade Center
New York
412 metres

Sears Tower
Chicago
475 metres

Tokyo Tower
333 metres

Television Tower
Moscow
537 metres

Eiffel Tower
Paris
321 metres

Radio Tower
Warsaw
646 metres

Empire State Building
New York
449 metres

There are many other famous places in Paris

Paris is the capital of France. The River Seine flows through the city. On the Right Bank are the Champs-Élysées, the Louvre Museum, Montmartre and the Opera House. On the Left Bank are the University and student quarter, and the Eiffel Tower. The Cathedral of Notre Dame stands on an island in the River Seine.

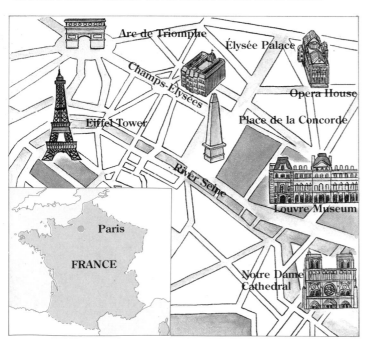

▲ **Arc de Triomphe.** Monument to Napoleon's armies.

▲ **Paris Opera House.** Symbol of French culture.

❓ Who Made the Palace of Versailles a Famous Place?

ANSWER It was King Louis XIV of France who made Versailles famous. He rebuilt it and filled its rooms with beautiful paintings and furniture. The area round the palace was turned into lovely gardens with lots of fountains and statues. Today, France is no longer ruled by a king but this old palace is still very famous.

▶ **Louis XIV's bedroom.** The walls were decorated with real gold. Louis XIV spared no expense to make his home magnificent.

▼ **Outside.** The beautiful gardens that surround the royal palace at Versailles were carefully planned. In front of the palace is a statue of Louis XIV on his horse.

Royal chapel. The floor of this room is covered with beautiful marble designs. It was here that Louis XVI married Marie Antoinette in 1770.

The Queen's Salon. This is where the queen met her guests. She entertained foreign visitors as well as French lords and ladies.

Salon of War. This room celebrates the victories of the king's armies. A plaster relief on the wall shows him riding his horse into battle.

Salon of Peace. This room was used by the queens of France as a music room. They also used it as a private place where they could read or just pass the time quietly.

Hall of Mirrors. This enormous and splendid gallery has 17 windows overlooking the gardens. Opposite the windows are 17 false "windows" made up of more than 500 mirrors.

● **To the Parent**

Versailles was used as a hunting lodge by Louis XIII. Louis XIV, nicknamed the "Sun King", transformed it into a magnificent palace surrounded by large formal gardens. It was seen as a symbol of royal extravagance until the French Revolution and the downfall of King Louis XVI. In 1837, Louis-Philippe restored the palace and made it into a museum.

What Is So Unusual About These Cave Paintings?

ANSWER These paintings, in a cave at Lascaux in France, were done by Stone Age people called Cro-Magnons as long as 25,000 years ago. On the cave walls are about 100 drawings of various animals, one of them an ox-like beast called an aurochs. Some of the paintings are six metres high and many of them show that the artists were very skilful.

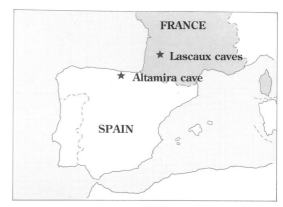

▼ The Lascaux paintings are very lifelike.

◄ **Man and animals**
Outside the caves ►

■ How were they done?

The cave dwellers used coloured clays and charcoal, and painted the pictures with their fingers. To light the caves they burnt animal fat in stone lamps.

Four young boys lost their dog while they were out playing in a field. They thought it might have fallen into a small hole they discovered in the grass. They dug at the hole to make it big enough for them to squeeze through.

They were amazed at what they found inside. They were in a big cave. But not just an ordinary cave. Its walls were covered with marvellous pictures. And the boys found their little dog too! This all happened in 1940.

Paintings at Altamira in Spain

Caves at Altamira also contain many paintings. In an area that extends from southwest France to northern Spain there are a great many caverns that have ancient wall paintings. Some also have sculptures. When the first paintings were found in 1879, no one believed they were so old. But since then, studies have shown that they are very old indeed.

Altamira painting ▶

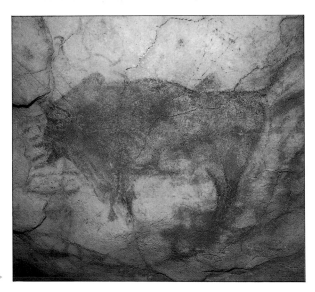

● **To the Parent**

The Lascaux cave's drawings of horses, deer and bison, which had been the cave dwellers' main source of food, became a major tourist attraction. But that brought pollution. By the early 1960s scientists noticed algae on some paintings. They decided that the problem had been caused by the humidity of exhaled breath in the cave. In 1963 the cave was closed to avoid further damage to the paintings. But in another cave, which was named Lascaux 2, scientifically exact replicas of the cave art were painted, and Lascaux 2 is open to the public on most days of the year. At Altamira, in northern Spain, replica works of art are also on display to avoid damage to the original paintings.

? Why Is Venice Called the City of Canals?

ANSWER Venice is a famous city in northern Italy. It was built long ago on 118 small islands. Canals run between the different parts of the city. To get from place to place, people usually travel by boat. The islands are also connected by more than 400 bridges. Tourists love to visit this unusual city.

Venice

ITALY

Rome

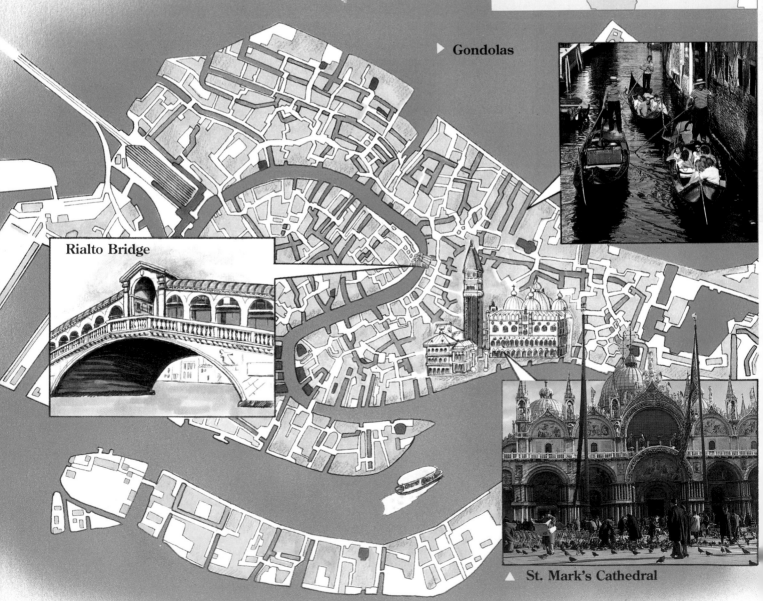

▶ Gondolas

Rialto Bridge

▲ St. Mark's Cathedral

■ The gondolas of Venice

Boats called gondolas are often used by visitors to Venice. But the people who live there travel by canal bus or motorboat. They use these in much the same way that people in other cities use cars and buses. Private motorboats are tied up in front of the houses.

◀ Gondolas gliding along one of the big canals.

❓ But Where Do the Cars Go?

People don't drive cars in Venice. The few streets the city has are too narrow and twisting to drive along. Bicycles are not much use either because Venice has a great many bridges across its canals and these have too many steps for people to get over them with bicycles.

So boats are really the best way to travel around in Venice. The canal system works just like the road networks in other cities. People go to work or shopping or to the cinema by taking a motorboat or one of the canal buses. To them this way of travelling seems ordinary.

19

❓ Why Does the Tower of Pisa Lean?

▲ The marble tower is 56 metres high.

ANSWER This is one of the world's most famous buildings. It was begun in 1174 and took about 180 years to build. After the first three storeys were built the ground beneath the tower started to sink. That made the tower lean over. The engineers who measure the tower say it leans a little more all the time — about a centimetre every 10 years

Oh! It looks as if it's going to fall over! I hope it doesn't land on me.

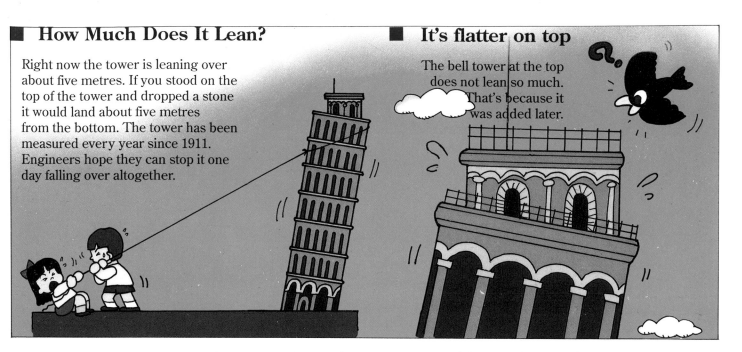

■ How Much Does It Lean?

Right now the tower is leaning over about five metres. If you stood on the top of the tower and dropped a stone it would land about five metres from the bottom. The tower has been measured every year since 1911. Engineers hope they can stop it one day falling over altogether.

■ It's flatter on top

The bell tower at the top does not lean so much. That's because it was added later.

Galileo and the tower

Galileo Galilei was a scientist who was born in Pisa in 1564. Legend says that Galileo dropped two balls, one 100 times as heavy as the other, from the top of the tower at the same time to show that both would hit the ground together. Whether he really did this or not, Galileo's careful experiments showed that it was only the resistance of the air that prevented objects of different weights falling at exactly the same speed. It is also said that he discovered the principle of a pendulum's swing by watching swaying chandeliers.

● **To the Parent**

The science of dynamics had made very little, if any, progress from Aristotle's time until Galileo's. It was thought that if two objects, one 10 times as heavy as the other, were dropped together the lighter would take 10 times as long to hit the ground. It wasn't realized that when a light object fell more slowly than a heavy one this was due to air resistance. The credit for proving this point went to Galileo, although similar experiments had been conducted in Holland during Galileo's time by Simon Stevin, a Dutch physicist.

❓ How Old Is the Roman Colosseum?

ANSWER The Colosseum was built about 1,900 years ago. The people of ancient Rome came to this great arena to watch ceremonies, fights and other events. Much of the Colosseum is still standing today.

▲ The outside of the Colosseum

■ Inside the ruins

The Colosseum shows that the ancient Romans were very skilful builders. The huge arena is not round but oval. It measures about 200 metres long, 170 metres wide and 50 metres high. The Colosseum's four levels could hold more than 48,000 people.

■ Here gladiators fought wild beasts

ITALY

● Rome

The ancient Romans came to the Colosseum to watch men fight with wild animals. At the opening ceremonies in about 80 A.D., fights were held for 100 days. Large numbers of gladiators and animals were killed.

Some of the Colosseum's special features

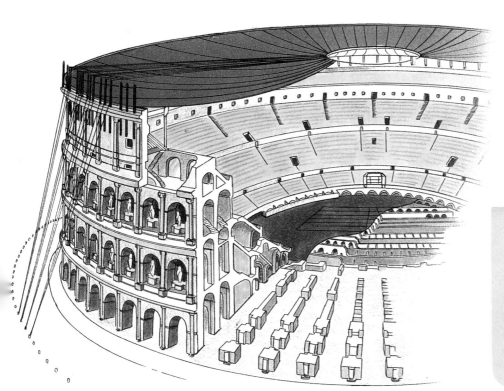

Canvas tents were built to shelter the spectators from sun or rain while they watched the fighting. The centre of the arena could be flooded, and then water battles were held. Corridors on two levels led into the Colosseum from outside, so that crowds of people could get to their seats quickly.

? Why Are the Ruins at Pompeii So Famous?

ANSWER Pompeii was a large city in ancient Italy. It had many shops and was a busy, bustling place. In 79 A.D., Mount Vesuvius, a volcano near the city, erupted and Pompeii was destroyed. In modern times, people discovered the ruins of Pompeii, buried under eight metres of ash. What they found let them see what life had been like there long ago.

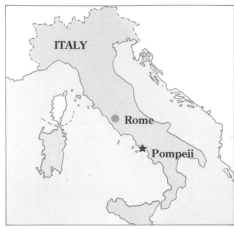

▼ **Main street**
Pompeii's roads were orderly and paved. Each house in this ancient city had its own water supply.

▲ **Public baths**

Amphitheatre ▶

● **To the Parent**

The city of Pompeii was colonized by the Romans in about 100 B.C., though it had been a Roman ally at one point, probably against its will. Little seems to have been written about Pompeii, even by the Roman writer Pliny the Elder, who died trying to rescue friends at Stabiae during the eruption. Most of what we know of Pompeii's past has been gleaned from study of the excavations. An isolated villa named Oplontis, also buried by the volcano, was not discovered until 1964.

■ The city of Pompeii

Pompeii was surrounded by a wall. Inside the city there are market squares, temples, amphitheatres and public baths as well as many handsome houses.

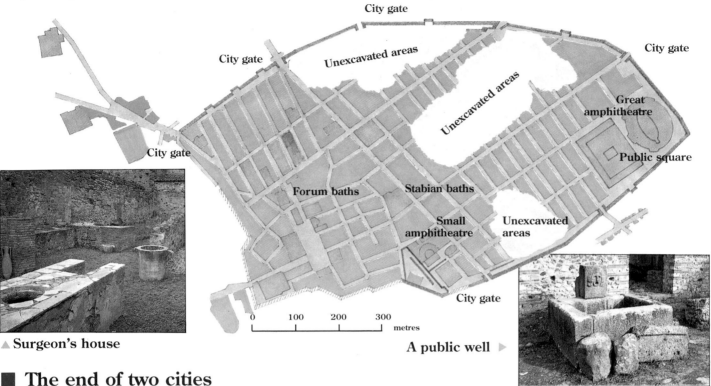

▲ **Surgeon's house**

A public well ▶

■ The end of two cities

Not only Pompeii was destroyed. Herculaneum 14.5 kilometres away was buried by lava. An earthquake 17 years earlier had wrecked both cities, and they had not recovered when Vesuvius erupted.

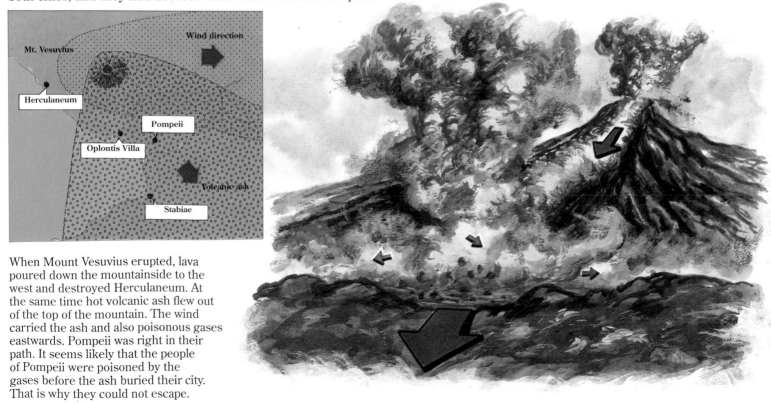

When Mount Vesuvius erupted, lava poured down the mountainside to the west and destroyed Herculaneum. At the same time hot volcanic ash flew out of the top of the mountain. The wind carried the ash and also poisonous gases eastwards. Pompeii was right in their path. It seems likely that the people of Pompeii were poisoned by the gases before the ash buried their city. That is why they could not escape.

Which Is the World's Smallest Country?

ANSWER Vatican City is the smallest country in the world. It is only 0.44 square kilometres in size. The Pope, who is head of the Roman Catholic Church, and about 1,500 people live there. Vatican City is in the centre of Rome. It has been an independent state since 1929.

ITALY

Vatican City

■ How big is it?

= 60

Vatican City is about the same size as 60 soccer fields put together.

◀ Crowds gather in St. Peter's Square.

▼ Here is the square seen from the air.

■ Inside the Vatican City

In addition to St. Peter's Basilica, the most impressive Catholic church in the world, and the Papal Palace, the Vatican City has its own museum, a broadcasting station, newspaper offices and a railway station. Although an independent state, it is easily entered from Rome.

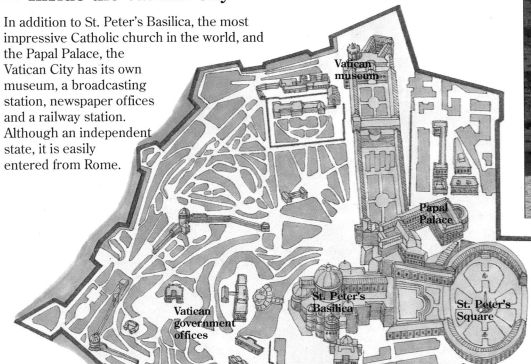

Vatican City is guarded by soldiers known as the Swiss Guards. Their brightly coloured uniforms were designed by the great Italian artist Michelangelo, whose paintings decorate many of the buildings here.

The five smallest countries

Despite their size these small countries each have special features that make them very popular with tourists.

If these five tiny independent countries were all put together their total land area wouldn't cover an area even one-sixth the size of London.

1 **Vatican City**
0.44 km²

2 **Monaco**
1.9 km²

3 **Nauru**
21 km²

4 **San Marino**
62 km²

5 **Liechtenstein**
160 km²

● **To the Parent**

Although it is an independent state the Vatican City issues no passports. There is no tax on goods entering or leaving, and its currency is the same as that used in the rest of Italy. As head of the Roman Catholic Church, the Pope has absolute authority in Vatican City. One reason why people from all over the world come here is to see paintings, sculptures and other famous works of art from the Vatican's collection.

❓ Why Did the Greeks Build the Parthenon?

ANSWER The Parthenon was built more than 2,400 years ago. The Greeks built this temple to honour the goddess Athena. It was believed that she protected the city of Athens from harm. Today, the ruins of the Parthenon are still standing.

▼ The Parthenon

The goddess Athena

The ancient Greeks believed she was a goddess with special powers to protect the city of Athens from harm. When the Parthenon was built on the Acropolis, a fortified hill overlooking the city, a large statue of her stood at its centre.

The Pride of Athens

Ancient Greece was made up of
a number of city-states. The
greatest of these was Athens, which
was built around a tall hill called
the Acropolis. There were several
other important buildings, but the
dominant feature on the Acropolis
was the temple dedicated to Athena.

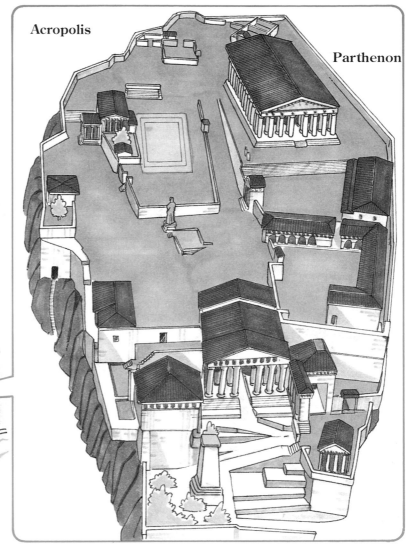

Acropolis

Parthenon

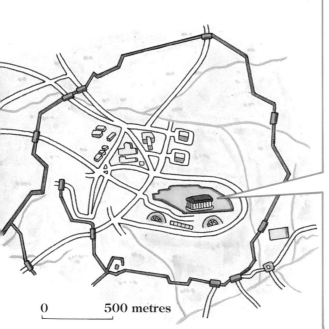

0   500 metres

How Did They Build Those Tall Columns?

The Parthenon's huge
columns rise to a height
of 10 metres. Each
column is made from
a number of round
carved stones piled
one on top of another.
Wooden or metal
wedges in the centre
of the columns keep
the stones in place.

● To the Parent

Athens was the city-state that held
the position of leadership in ancient
Greece. The Acropolis stood at the
centre of the city, and the Parthenon
was its focal point. It is said to be
the great masterpiece of the ancient
Greeks' culture. Over the years the
Parthenon's fortunes have varied. It
is said to have been a Christian place
of worship at one point in history. It
became an armoury when Ottoman Turks
invaded Greece more than a millennium
later. It has suffered from pollution
caused by exhaust fumes and smog in
recent years, but restoration work is
in progress and seems to be working.

What Are Fjords and How Are They Formed?

ANSWER Fjords are long, narrow bodies of water. They are formed by glaciers. These rivers of moving ice cut deep valleys in the mountains. When the ice melts the sea moves in and fills them with water. Norway is famous for its many beautiful fjords.

Geiranger Fjord, Norway ▶

■ How fjords are made

The mountains are entirely covered by glaciers.

The glaciers start moving slowly down the valleys.

And What Causes These Glaciers?

High mountains and cold places such as the Arctic and Antarctic are covered by snow all the year round. The snow never melts. As more snow falls on top of the snow that has already settled, layers upon layers pile up. The snow at the bottom is crushed into ice and forms glaciers. The glaciers slide slowly down the mountainsides like huge rivers of ice.

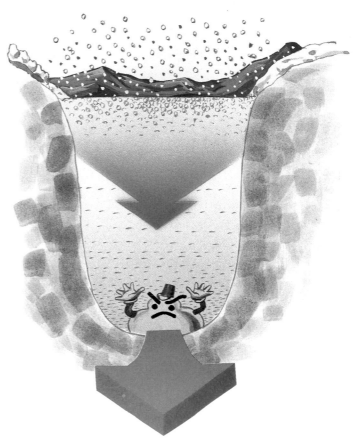

Over thousands of years the moving glaciers wear away valley walls. When the glaciers melt the sea rushes in.

● **To the Parent**

Fjords are common geological features along the coasts of Scandinavia. They are long, narrow and deep inlets enclosed on either side by sheer, high cliffs. Fjords are formed by glacial erosion. Glaciers that are the accumulation of tens of thousands of years of snowfall in the mountains are called valley glaciers. Glaciers that form on level surfaces, such as those in the polar ice, are called continental glaciers. These rivers of ice move at a speed of from two centimetres to more than a metre a day. Their force is vastly greater than that of any river, and they easily slice away the sides of valleys as they move through them. Glacial erosion formed many of the natural scenic wonders found in the world.

31

❓ What Kind of Place Is the Kremlin?

ANSWER The Kremlin is built on a hill in Moscow, the capital of the U.S.S.R. "Kremlin" is the Russian word for a fortress, and the Kremlin in Moscow has a strong wall built all round it. Inside the Kremlin are many government buildings, and also a number of monuments, museums and cathedrals which tourists like to visit.

▼ **Cathedral of the Annunciation**

▼ **Great Kremlin Palace**

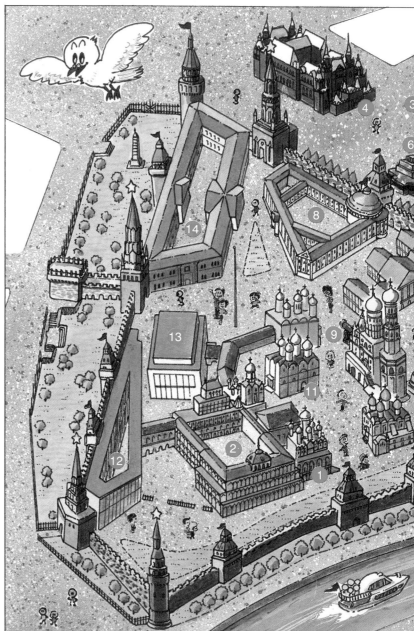

1. Cathedral of the Annunciation 2. Great Kremlin Palace 3. Red Square 4. State of St. Basil 6. Lenin's Tomb 7. Redeemer Tower 8. Council of Ministers Building 11. Cathedral of the Assumption 12. Armoury 13. Palace of Congresses 14. Arsenal

▲ Red Square

ical Museum 5. Cathedral
ar Cannon 10. Tsar Bell
UM Department Store

▲ State Historical Museum

▲ Cathedral of St. Basil

■ Tsar Bell and Tsar Cannon

This bell weighs 180 tonnes and the cannon weighs 38 tonnes. They have never been used.

Ugh! It's heavy!

So is this!

● To the Parent

Citadels known as kremlins were built in the centre of many Russian cities during the Middle Ages. Many survive today in cities across the U.S.S.R., but the best known is the Kremlin in Moscow. The government of the U.S.S.R., the Supreme Soviet, is housed in the Great Kremlin Palace. Although many people believe that it's impossible to get inside the Kremlin, the fact is that many tourists visit it every day. Many artefacts from the tsarist era are on display there.

❓ Why Is the Statue of Liberty in New York Harbour?

ANSWER The Statue of Liberty is a symbol of freedom and also of friendship. It was a gift to the United States from the people of France. It was their way of remembering the help France gave to America during the American War of Independence. The statue has been standing in New York harbour since 1886.

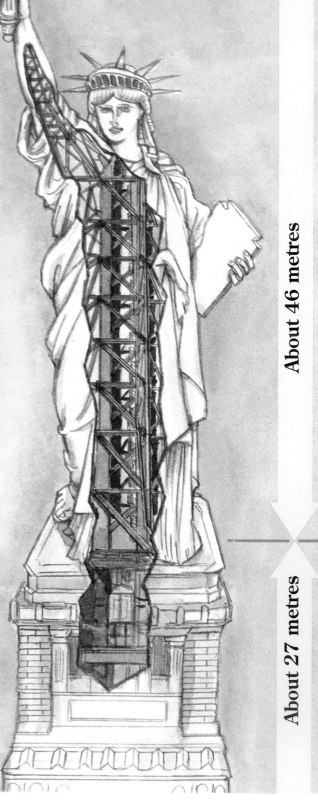

About 46 metres

About 27 metres

▼ The Statue of Liberty, soaring 92 metres above the harbour, has greeted visitors to America's shores for more than 100 years.

The Statue Was Designed and Built in France

The Statue of Liberty commemorates the friendship and aid that France gave America when America was fighting for its independence from Britain in the 1770s. Only France sent troops to help. The drawings show how the statue was assembled.

Next, he made another model one quarter of the full size. This was enlarged to produce the final statue.

Sculptor Frédéric-Auguste Bartholdi first made a small clay model. Then he made a larger one three metres high.

Using the model, the statue was cast in copper.

The finished statue, weighing 200 tonnes, was then shipped in sections to New York on a French ship. It took several years to assemble.

The head was the last piece.

Supported by a steel frame to prevent warping, the copper sections were fitted back together and placed on a base that the Americans had built.

● To the Parent

In the century since its dedication the statue had become the symbol of America, and it had also deteriorated badly. With public donations it was refurbished, and on its centennial Chief Justice Warren E. Burger swore in 5,000 new Americans on Liberty Island, while all across the land 20,000 other new citizens were sworn in simultaneously in a satellite telecast.

What Would You See in America's National Parks?

ANSWER America has many huge national parks. They are areas of great natural beauty or special historic interest that have been set aside for everyone to enjoy. Here are some of the things you would be able to see.

▲ **Yosemite: California.** Visitors here see Yosemite Falls, the second highest waterfall in the world. There are giant redwood trees in the park that are many centuries old.

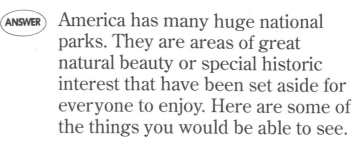
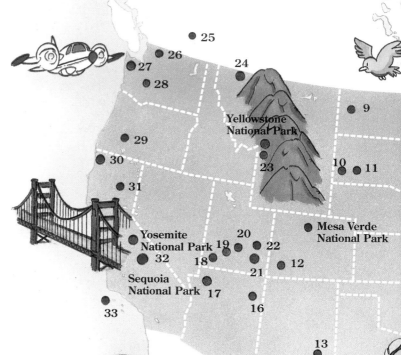

▲ **Sequoia: California.** Here are the giant sequoias, which are a species of redwood and are among the world's oldest and largest living things. Many are 3,000 to 4,000 years old, and some have a diameter of more than nine metres.

■ National treasures

The national parks of America are scattered from Alaska to Hawaii and the American Virgin Islands. The United States Congress decides which areas will be made into national parks. At present there are about 50. Millions of people get pleasure from these parks, and they are great national treasures.

◀ Yellowstone: Wyoming, Montana, and Idaho

This was America's first national park and is its largest.
It has 10,000 geysers, including the famous Old Faithful.
It is rich in wildlife, lakes, rivers and waterfalls. But
in 1988 fires destroyed thousands of hectares of park woodland,
and it could be many years before new timber can grow back.

Mesa Verde: Colorado

This park was established in 1906
to save some important prehistoric
cliff dwellings. They were the homes
of the Pueblo Indians long before
Columbus made his voyage to America.
The park is noted for its rugged scenery.

Everglades
National Park

▲ Everglades: Florida.

This park is a huge marsh.
It is famous for its plants and wildlife. Visitors
here can see a number of endangered species
including crocodiles, alligators and bald eagles.

Acadia	17. Grand Canyon
Shenandoah	18. Zion
Biscayne	19. Bryce Canyon
Great Smokies	20. Capitol Reef
Hot Springs	21. Canyonlands
Mammoth Cave	22. Arches
Isle Royale	23. Ground Teton
Voyageurs	24. Glacier
Theodore Roosevelt	25. Mount Revelstoke
Wind Cave	26. North Cascades
Badlands	27. Olympic
Rocky Mountains	28. Mount Rainier
Carlsbad Caverns	29. Crater Lake
Guadaloupe	30. Redwood
Mountains	31. Lassen Volcanic
Big Bend	32. Kings Canyon
Petrified Forest	33. Channel Islands

● To the Parent

America's national parks are vast. Yellowstone National Park
alone is almost twice as large as the state of Delaware. It
is impossible to cover most of them on foot. To see the sights
visitors usually travel by car or bus, or in some cases by
aeroplane or helicopter. Notices and directional signs in the
parks use international symbols as well as English to make it
easier for visitors from other countries to find their way around.

How Was the Grand Canyon Formed?

(ANSWER) The Grand Canyon in Arizona is about 350 kilometres long and up to 1,620 metres deep in some places. The sides of this huge canyon were worn away by the Colorado River. It took millions of years for the canyon to get so big. Today, the river is still wearing away the rock little by little.

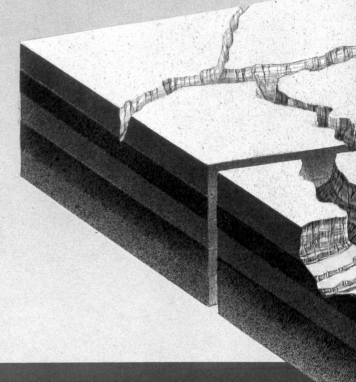

▼ **The Grand Canyon**

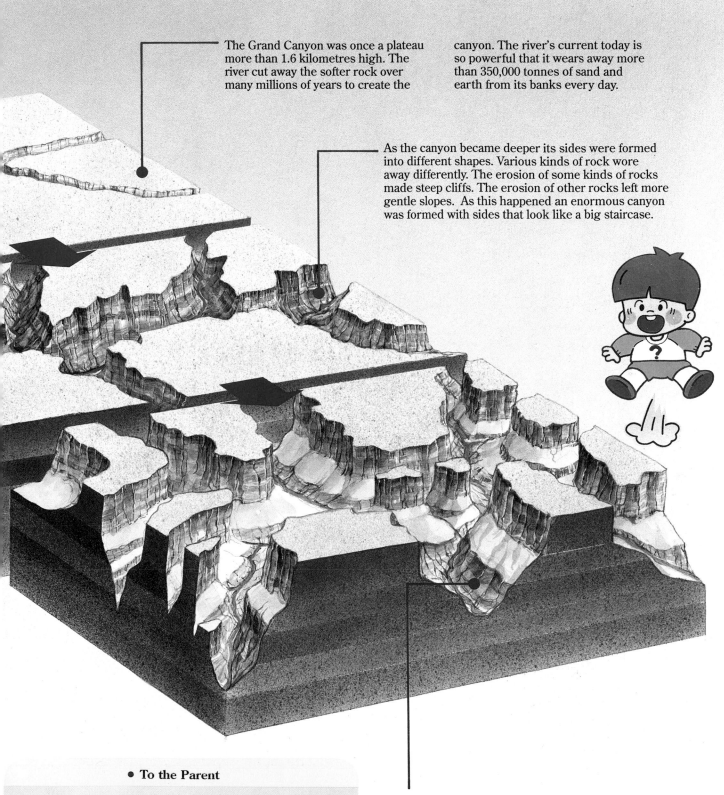

The Grand Canyon was once a plateau more than 1.6 kilometres high. The river cut away the softer rock over many millions of years to create the canyon. The river's current today is so powerful that it wears away more than 350,000 tonnes of sand and earth from its banks every day.

As the canyon became deeper its sides were formed into different shapes. Various kinds of rock wore away differently. The erosion of some kinds of rocks made steep cliffs. The erosion of other rocks left more gentle slopes. As this happened an enormous canyon was formed with sides that look like a big staircase.

● To the Parent

The Grand Canyon is an area of magnificent scenery and is perhaps the best known of all of America's national parks. The canyon itself is a massive gorge. Scenic trails, usually taken by mule train, lead from the top down into the canyon. Fossils revealed in layers of exposed rock strata along the sides of the canyon include conifer needles, dragonflies, and even sharks, which offer positive evidence that this area has been both seabed and mountaintop at different times. The Grand Canyon is a magnificent example of artistry in nature while revealing some of the ways that nature works.

The walls of the Grand Canyon are made up of many layers of rock. By studying these layers scientists have learnt a great deal. They have discovered many types of fossils in the canyon's walls. At the bottom are fossils of ocean life which are about 570 million years old. Higher up are fossils of ferns which are about 280 million years old. The walls of the canyon are a museum of earth's history.

Whose Faces Are Carved on Mount Rushmore?

ANSWER They are faces of four of America's greatest presidents — George Washington, Thomas Jefferson, Abraham Lincoln and Theodore Roosevelt — carved into the mountain. This famous monument is in South Dakota. Every year more than a million tourists visit it.

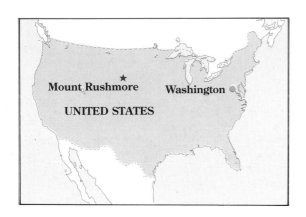

National memorial ▶

The four presidents *(left to right)* are George Washington, Thomas Jefferson, Theodore Roosevelt and Abraham Lincoln.

What Did Each of These Four Presidents Do?

George Washington (1732-1799)

He led the American people to victory in the War of Independence. He was elected the first president of the new nation.

Thomas Jefferson (1743-1826)

He was the author of the American Declaration of Independence. He was a wealthy farmer and studied law before he became president.

■ Monumental

The head of Washington is about
18 metres high. Made to the same scale,
a complete statue of the first president
would be about 142 metres high.

18 metres

● To the Parent

The sculptor Gutzon Borglum began work
on the mammoth project at Mount
Rushmore in 1927. But it was frequently
delayed by bad weather and a lack of money.
The entire project took more than 14 years
to complete. Borglum himself didn't live
to see the work finished, but his son,
Lincoln, completed the project for him.

Abraham Lincoln (1809-1865)

One of his promises to the American people
when he was elected was to end slavery. He was
president during the American Civil War.

Theodore Roosevelt (1858-1919)

He supported laws to help protect ordinary
people from the powers of big business. He also
set aside large areas of land for conservation.

41

What Is the Origin of the Petrified Forest?

ANSWER Millions of years ago, much of Arizona was covered with forest. Over time, trees fell down and were buried under gravel and sand. As more time passed, a natural process turned the buried tree to stone. When this happens to things we say they become petrified. Later, when wind and water wore away the ground covering them, a huge area of petrified trees could be seen.

▶ Fossilized trees lie where they fell many millions of years ago. Now they are stone.

How nature turns trees into stone

About 200 million years ago the land around eastern Arizona looked very different. It was covered by a vast forest of trees, such as pines and cedars, and ferns.

When the trees died they fell to the ground. They were then swept away in flooded streams. The dead trees lodged in the gravel and sand of the stream beds.

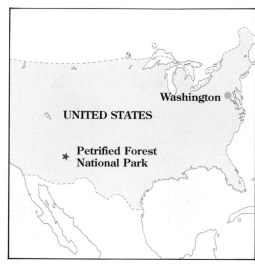

● **To the Parent**

The Petrified Forest is in a corner of an area called the Painted Desert. It is believed that the trees were fossilized because of the nature of the soil where they were buried. It retarded decay and allowed time for the trees to petrify. The process replaces the natural wood fibres with silica. The process is often so accurate that the structure of the tree, inside and out, is just like the original.

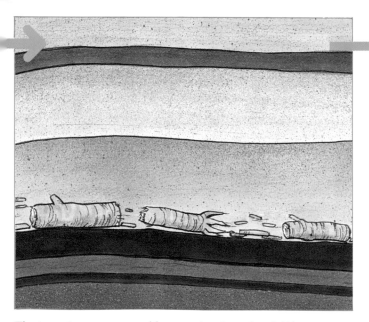

The trees became covered by gravel and sand and did not rot away. Instead, as more sand piled up, the wood was replaced by minerals. The trees slowly turned to stone.

Then, over millions of years, the material surrounding the stone tree trunks was washed away. The petrified trees were left lying on the surface where we can see them today.

? How Can Big Ships Get Through the Panama Canal?

ANSWER This canal joins the Atlantic and Pacific Oceans. It is made up of a series of giant water tanks called locks. Locks can connect two bodies of water that are at different levels. When the ship enters a lock, water is added or taken away in order to raise or lower the ship. Ships coming from the Atlantic are raised so that they can cross Gatun Lake, in the centre of the Panama Canal.

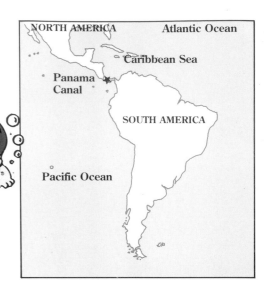

Enlarged plan of Gatun

1 Ships entering the canal from the Caribbean Sea on the Atlantic Ocean side enter lock A, and the gates are closed. The water level inside is the same as sea level. Lock B is higher than sea level, so valves in the pipes are opened and water from lock B pours into lock A. This makes the water levels in both locks the same and raises the ship. Gate A is opened and the ship moves into lock B.

▲ An oceangoing cargo ship enters the canal. Large ships are towed through the canal by locomotive engines.

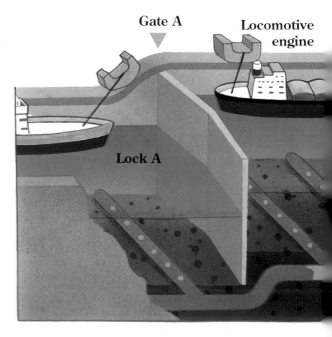

● **To the Parent**

While the Panama Canal has locks, the Suez Canal has none since it is at the same level as the sea along its 160-kilometre length. Canals can greatly shorten shipping routes. The Suez Canal trims 8,800 kilometres off the distance between London and India. The Panama Canal cuts the distance between Pacific Ocean ports and the Caribbean by about 13,000 kilometres.

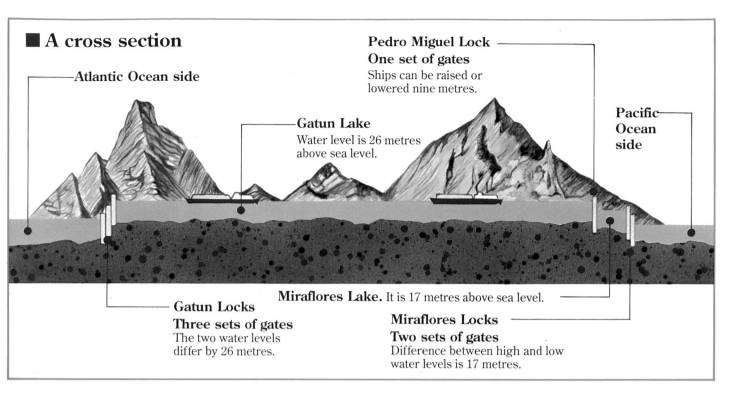

■ A cross section

Atlantic Ocean side

Pedro Miguel Lock — **One set of gates**
Ships can be raised or lowered nine metres.

Pacific Ocean side

Gatun Lake
Water level is 26 metres above sea level.

Gatun Locks
Three sets of gates
The two water levels differ by 26 metres.

Miraflores Lake. It is 17 metres above sea level. —

Miraflores Locks —
Two sets of gates
Difference between high and low water levels is 17 metres.

Locks

2 When the ship is in lock B, gate A is closed and valves in the next section of pipes are opened. The water level and the ship in lock B are both raised to the same height as the water level of lock C. Gate B opens and the ship moves into lock C.

3 Valves in the final section of pipes are opened to raise the water in lock C to the same level as Gatun Lake. Gate C opens and the ship can then proceed across the lake. Because of the time spent passing through the locks, it takes a ship about eight hours to go through the canal.

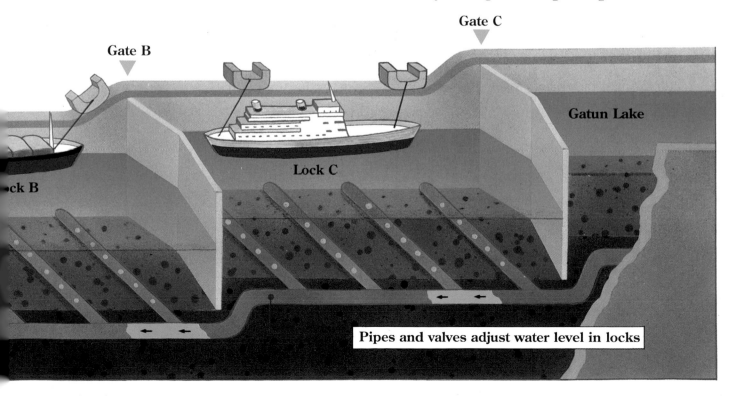

Gate C

Gate B

Gatun Lake

Lock C

ck B

Pipes and valves adjust water level in locks

What Waterfall Is the Highest?

ANSWER The tallest waterfall is in South America. Angel Falls on the upper Caroni River in Venezuela drops 979 metres. It is in an area of thick tropical rain forest and is named after James Angel, an American pilot. He had to make a forced landing in his plane there in 1937 and discovered the waterfall by chance.

■ The waterfall makes a spectacular drop in stages from the Plateau of Guyana. Its highest single fall is 807 metres.

979 metres

●To the Parent

Niagara Falls has two precipices, the higher of which is only 51 metres. But it is famous worldwide because, being on the border between the United States and Canada, it is easy to reach, and because a great volume of water rushes over the falls. On the other hand Angel Falls, which is almost 20 times as high as Niagara, gets few visitors because it takes a five-day boat trip to reach it.

How are waterfalls made?

1 Flowing lava from a volcano may block the upper waters of a river or a stream and cause a lake to be formed. Eventually, the water from the lake will overflow this natural dam. This creates a waterfall.

2 Part of a riverbed may be formed of harder rock that does not wear away as quickly as surrounding rock. The flowing river water cuts away the softer rock at a faster rate, and a waterfall is created.

3 A fast-flowing river may severely wear away and deepen its riverbed. A slower-moving branch of the river, unable to wear down its riverbed as quickly, will form a waterfall where it flows into the main river.

Did You Know That a Waterfall Can Move?

The force of the water flowing over Niagara Falls is so great that it wears away the base rock. The result is that the falls are moving farther up the river at a rate of about one metre every year.

▼ **Movement of Niagara Falls**

American side

Canadian side

2,000 ▶ years ago

◀ 4,000 years ago

12,000 ▶ years ago

About 10 kilometres

◀ **Sightseeing boats at Niagara Falls**

How a waterfall erodes rock

Previous position

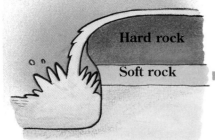

Hard rock

Soft rock

Water pouring over the rock splashes violently against the softer rock closer to the bottom of the falls.

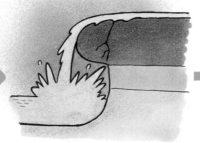

The water striking the lower rock gradually wears it away. This action may continue for millions of years.

With the lower rock eroded away the hard upper rock has no support and crumbles under its own weight.

47

? Did You Know There Is a Place Called The Lost City of the Andes?

ANSWER This ancient city, named Machu Picchu, is high in the Andes mountains in Peru. It was built hundreds of years ago by the Incas, who were famous for their skill as builders. Today, one can still see clearly what the city was like.

■ Plan of Machu Picchu

It was a very orderly city, with a temple and a main square.

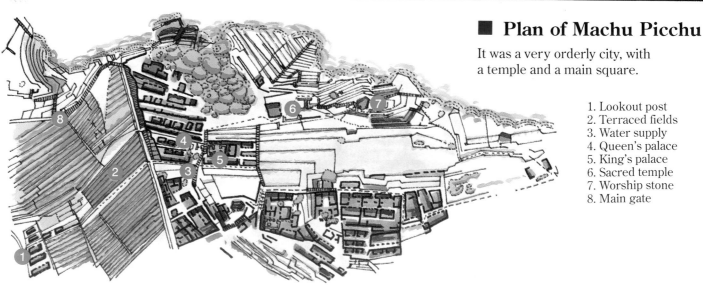

1. Lookout post
2. Terraced fields
3. Water supply
4. Queen's palace
5. King's palace
6. Sacred temple
7. Worship stone
8. Main gate

▲ This temple was dedicated to the queen and the sun.

The empire ruled by the Incas

The Incas had a mighty empire in South America long before anyone from Europe had ever been there. The centre of the Inca Empire was the city of Cuzco, in Peru. In the 16th century, the Inca Empire was conquered by Spanish invaders.

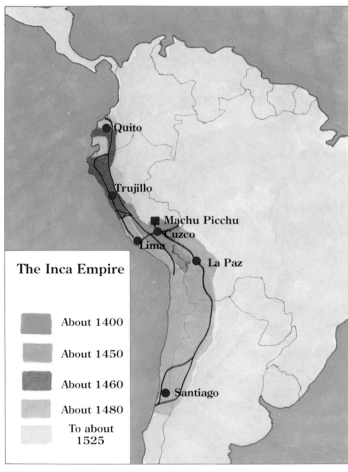

Quito

Trujillo

Machu Picchu
Cuzco
Lima

La Paz

The Inca Empire

About 1400

About 1450

About 1460

About 1480

To about
1525

Santiago

▲ These are ruins of dwellings used by ordinary people.

Inca culture: the two extremes

The Incas were very clever people and skilful builders. But they had no written language, so many things about them remain a mystery.

▲ Many roads were bordered by walls.

▲ They tied knots to leave messages.

● **To the Parent**

Machu Picchu is a major historical relic in almost perfect condition. There are various theories about Machu Picchu: that it was a main fortified base of the Inca Empire for the region of the Amazon; or that it was a city built for religious purposes; or that it was a secret city and its true purpose has yet to be discovered. Little remains to help us clear up the mysteries that surround Inca culture. There is no one living today who can even interpret the meaning of the knotted ropes, or quipus, they left behind.

What Are the Galápagos Islands Most Famous For?

ANSWER These islands are in the Pacific Ocean, far away from any other land. Their name comes from the Spanish word for a tortoise. The Galápagos Islands are famous for the unusual animals that live there. If you visited the islands you would see creatures unlike those found anywhere else in the world.

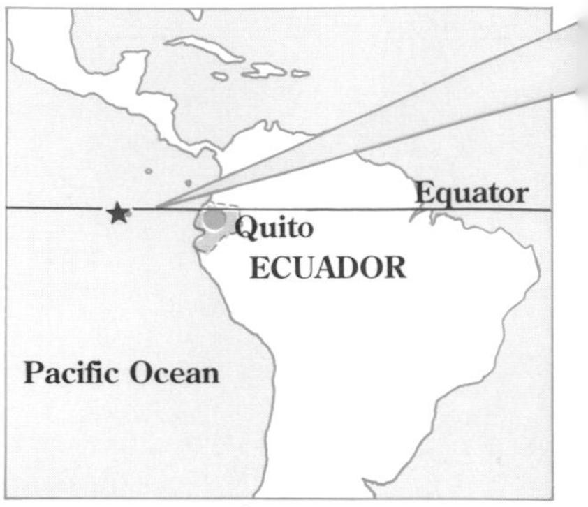

Equator
Quito
ECUADOR
Pacific Ocean

▶ **A frigate bird.** The male has a red crop or pouch on his neck. The female does not.

▼ **Land iguana.** This big reptile lives on the fleshy leaves of the cactus plant. It lies in the sun and seems to have no fear of humans.

▲ **Giant tortoise.** It is said that some of these big tortoises grow to weigh as much as 225 kilograms.

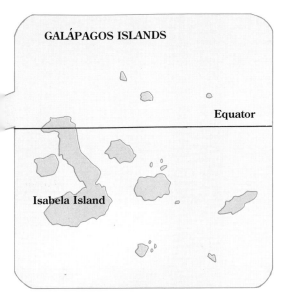

GALÁPAGOS ISLANDS

Equator

Isabela Island

Darwin and the Islands

Charles Darwin, a famous scientist, visited the Galápagos Islands and studied the animals he found there. Darwin's theory about how these and all other animal species developed over time is known as the "theory of evolution".

▲ **Charles Darwin**

■ The Galápagos Islands

Although they are on the equator, the Galápagos are washed by cold sea currents. Fresh water is scarce and the soil is rocky, so few plants grow there. There is a lot of volcanic activity on the islands.

The first finch on the Galápagos

■ Galápagos penguins

Penguins and seals can live in the Galápagos because currents keep the sea temperature down to about 15°C.

This one eats plants and grubs.

This one eats grubs off cactus plants.

This finch eats only plants.

▲ In the Galápagos there are finches that have beaks of different lengths according to what foods they eat. But it is believed that they all evolved from a single species over a long period of time. It is this process of evolution which Darwin set out to explain.

● **To the Parent**

Galápagos comes from the Spanish for tortoise, and the giant tortoise that is found only in the Galápagos is typical of the seemingly prehistoric creatures that inhabit the place. The marine iguana feeds on a species of seaweed that grows only there, so it is unique in the world. Although formidable in appearance, the creatures of the Galápagos neither fear nor attack humans. It is easy to understand how this place inspired Charles Darwin.

What Is the Mystery of Easter Island?

ANSWER Easter Island is in the South Pacific Ocean. On the island are hundreds of huge old stone statues with carved human faces. No one knows why they were made or who made them.

▼ **Easter Island statues.** One of the strangest things about them is that every one faces inland, away from the sea. Nearly all of them show only the body from the waist up.

How the Statues Were Made and Set in Place

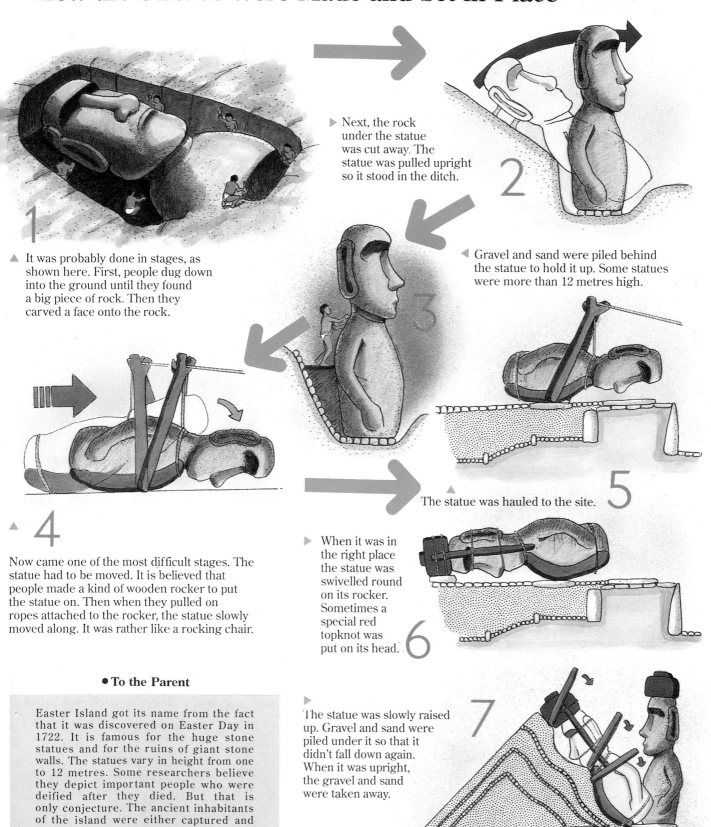

1 ▲ It was probably done in stages, as shown here. First, people dug down into the ground until they found a big piece of rock. Then they carved a face onto the rock.

2 ▷ Next, the rock under the statue was cut away. The statue was pulled upright so it stood in the ditch.

3 ◁ Gravel and sand were piled behind the statue to hold it up. Some statues were more than 12 metres high.

4 ▲ Now came one of the most difficult stages. The statue had to be moved. It is believed that people made a kind of wooden rocker to put the statue on. Then when they pulled on ropes attached to the rocker, the statue slowly moved along. It was rather like a rocking chair.

5 ▲ The statue was hauled to the site.

6 ▷ When it was in the right place the statue was swivelled round on its rocker. Sometimes a special red topknot was put on its head.

7 ▷ The statue was slowly raised up. Gravel and sand were piled under it so that it didn't fall down again. When it was upright, the gravel and sand were taken away.

● **To the Parent**

Easter Island got its name from the fact that it was discovered on Easter Day in 1722. It is famous for the huge stone statues and for the ruins of giant stone walls. The statues vary in height from one to 12 metres. Some researchers believe they depict important people who were deified after they died. But that is only conjecture. The ancient inhabitants of the island were either captured and enslaved or they died from diseases that were brought to the island on ships.

? What Is a Pyramid?

ANSWER The pyramids are in Egypt and were built long ago. In ancient times, Egypt was ruled by kings called pharaohs. These pyramids are the pharaohs' tombs. The Egyptians believed that someone who died would live again in another world. So they put in each pharaoh's tomb the things he would need in his next life.

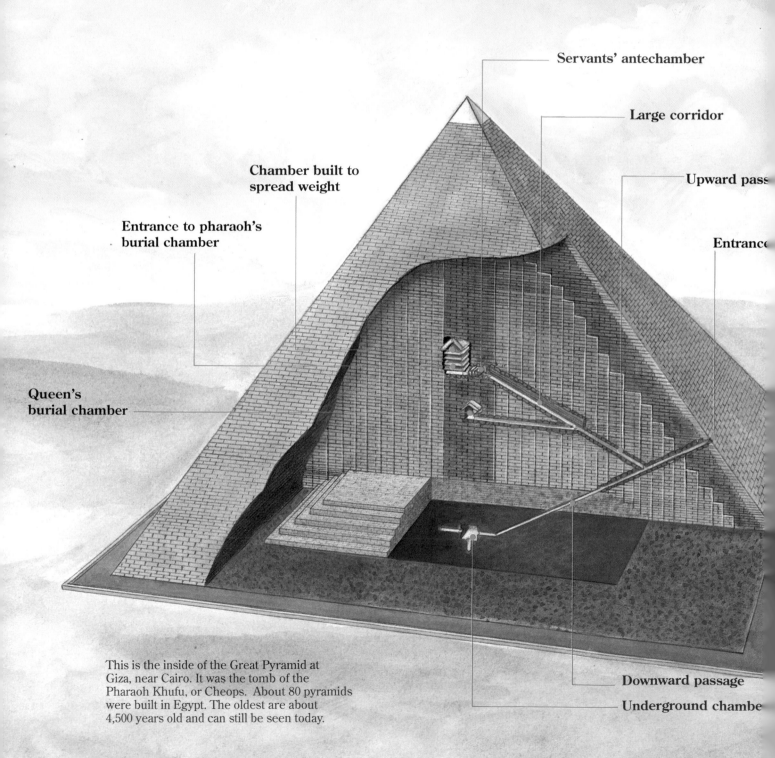

Servants' antechamber

Large corridor

Chamber built to spread weight

Upward pass

Entrance to pharaoh's burial chamber

Entrance

Queen's burial chamber

Downward passage

Underground chambe

This is the inside of the Great Pyramid at Giza, near Cairo. It was the tomb of the Pharaoh Khufu, or Cheops. About 80 pyramids were built in Egypt. The oldest are about 4,500 years old and can still be seen today.

The Sphinx, a mythical creature with a lion's body and human head, stands guard beside the pyramids.

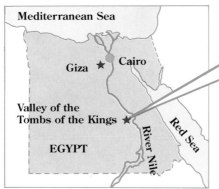

Mediterranean Sea

Giza ★ ● Cairo

Valley of the
Tombs of the Kings ★

EGYPT

River Nile

Red Sea

■ Valley of the tombs

About 60 tombs were built in a valley up the Nile from Cairo, called the Valley of the Tombs of the Kings.

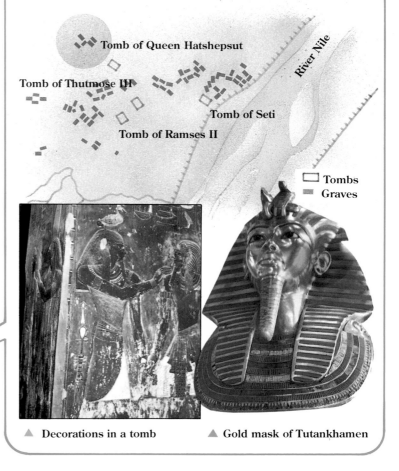

Tomb of Queen Hatshepsut

Tomb of Thutmose III

Tomb of Seti

Tomb of Ramses II

River Nile

☐ Tombs
▬ Graves

▲ Decorations in a tomb

▲ Gold mask of Tutankhamen

Great Tombs of the World

Throughout history, in many parts of the world, powerful rulers have ordered grand tombs to be built for themselves.
The great tombs are intended to remind the world of these rulers' greatness.

Pyramid of Pharaoh Khufu

About 147 metres high

230 metres

Imperial Tomb, Japan

35 metres high

486 metres

About 300 metres

About 684 metres

About 578 metres

Imperial tomb, China
About 50 metres high

● **To the Parent**

The pyramid of Pharaoh Khufu was built by fitting together more than 2,500,000 stone blocks, each of which weighed at least 2.5 tonnes. Construction took 25 years. The ancient Egyptians believed they would be reborn into the next world. Therefore, the pharaohs' bodies were carefully preserved and their splendid possessions were buried with them.

How Big Is the Sahara?

ANSWER The Sahara is the biggest desert in the world. It covers nearly a quarter of the whole African continent. It reaches into 12 countries. The desert measures 5,600 kilometres from east to west and 1,700 kilometres from north to south.

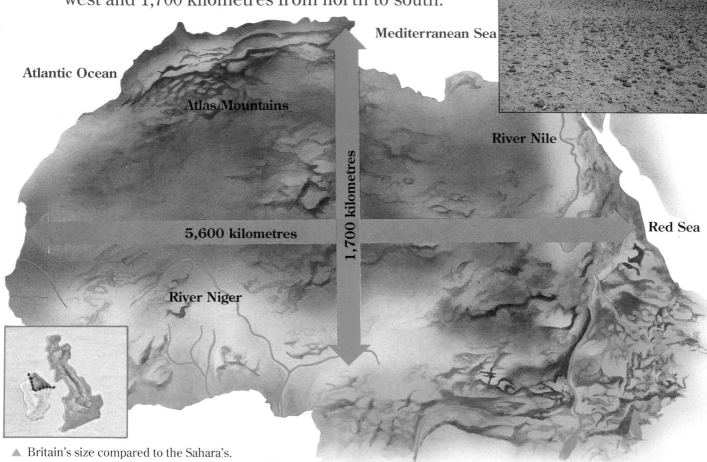

Atlantic Ocean

Mediterranean Sea

Atlas Mountains

River Nile

5,600 kilometres

1,700 kilometres

Red Sea

River Niger

▲ Britain's size compared to the Sahara's.

Animals of the Sahara

Like all deserts, the Sahara gets almost no rain. Because of this, very few animals and plants can live there. Those that do have developed special ways to survive in this hot, dry place. To be safe from the desert heat, many of the animals sleep all day in holes in the ground. Then they come out at night when it is cooler.

▲ **Horned viper.** It has an unusual way of getting to where it wants to go. It makes an S of its body and slithers across the sand sideways.

▲ **Sahara fox.** During the daytime it keeps cool in a hole tunnelled in a sand dune. It comes out only at night, when the hot sun has set.

Why Doesn't the Desert Get More Rainfall?

Dry air blows down over the desert

Most of the world's deserts are found in regions round the Tropics of Cancer and Capricorn, north and south of the equator. Dry air from the desert regions meets damp air coming from the equator and forms clouds. These clouds drop huge amounts of rain at the point where they are formed. But then, when it has lost its moisture, the dry air rises, curves round in a huge arc and drops back down to earth over the desert. The dry air has no more water to release on the desert as rain. And that is why deserts are such barren, dry places.

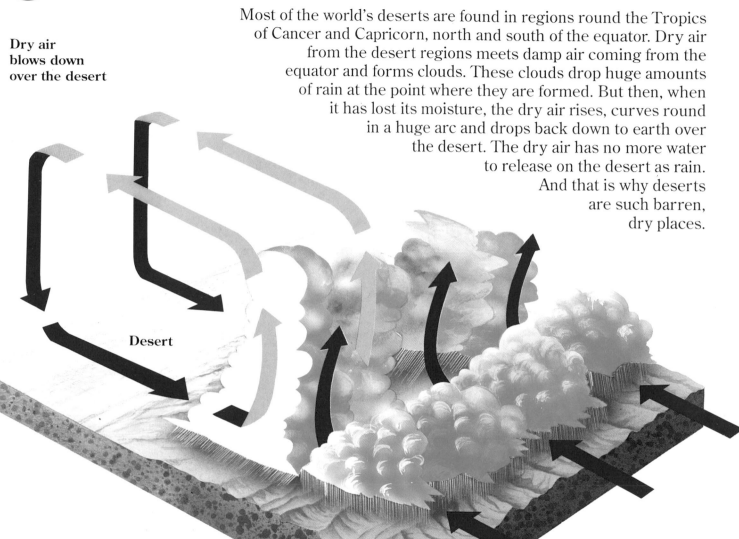

Desert

▲ **Desert scorpion.** In its tail it carries a deadly sting. After the sun has gone down it comes out to capture and kill insects to eat.

▲ **Jerboa.** Also called a jumping rat, it has powerful back legs to help it bound across the sand in leaps of 50 centimetres or more.

● **To the Parent**

The name "Sahara" is from the Arabic word meaning desert. This desert stretches from the Red Sea to the Atlantic Ocean, and it is larger than the Mediterranean Sea. Its very low rainfall does not encourage the growth of plants, although there are a few. Some animals also live in the desert — primarily small nocturnal ones, and a number of reptiles. The date palm, which can generally be found in and around oases, is one of the few plants that thrives, and a major source of food for the people whose home is the desert.

❓ Why Was the Aswan High Dam Built?

ANSWER Egypt is mostly desert. But there are some areas of farmland along the River Nile. In the past there was very little water in the river at some times of year. Then it would rain very heavily further up the river, causing floods. So a dam was built on the Nile at Aswan. In the rainy season it holds some of the water back to prevent flooding. In the dry season the water is released.

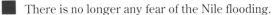
■ Since ancient times, the people of Egypt have had to worry about floods and about not being able to grow enough food. The Aswan High Dam has helped to end these problems and now farmers can grow crops all the year round.

■ There is no longer any fear of the Nile flooding.

Now with the dam I don't worry when it rains up river.

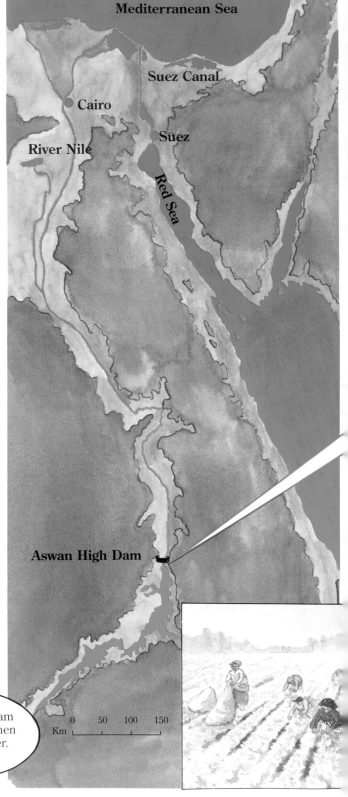

Mediterranean Sea

Suez Canal

Cairo

Suez

River Nile

Red Sea

Aswan High Dam

0   50   100   150
Km

■ The dam is also a source of electric power

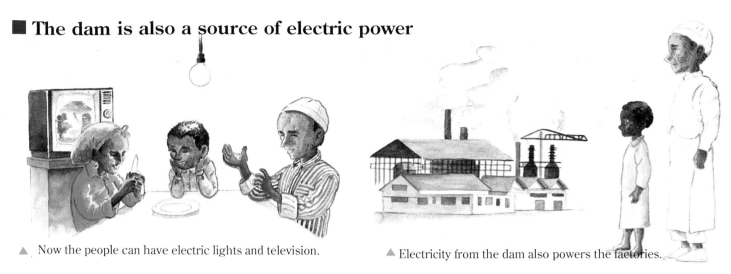

▲ Now the people can have electric lights and television.

▲ Electricity from the dam also powers the factories.

Aswan High Dam

Height: 110 metres

Thickness: 1,300 metres

Length: 3.5 kilometres

Capacity: 164,000 million cubic metres

■ The Nile's water level stays the same

The water level of the River Nile used to change greatly from season to season. Sometimes it would rise six metres or more in the rainy season. Now with the dam controlling the flow the water level stays the same.

● **To the Parent**

The Nile river basin holds many treasures from ancient Egypt. The construction of the Aswan High Dam threatened the survival of some of them. An artificial lake 600 kilometres long was formed when the dam was built. Two temples at Abu Simbel would have been covered by the waters of this lake. These temples date from the reign of Ramses II in the 13th century B.C. and are of great cultural importance. But under the supervision of the United Nations Educational, Scientific and Cultural Organization they were moved to higher ground.

What Was the Silk Road?

ANSWER The Silk Road was an ancient route that linked China with Europe. Along this road traders carried China's famous product, silk. They sold it in the markets of Italy, France and other European countries. The Silk Road was about 6,400 kilometres long, with many offshoots. Much of it crossed the deserts of the Middle East. Through the travellers on this road people in Europe and Asia began to learn about each other.

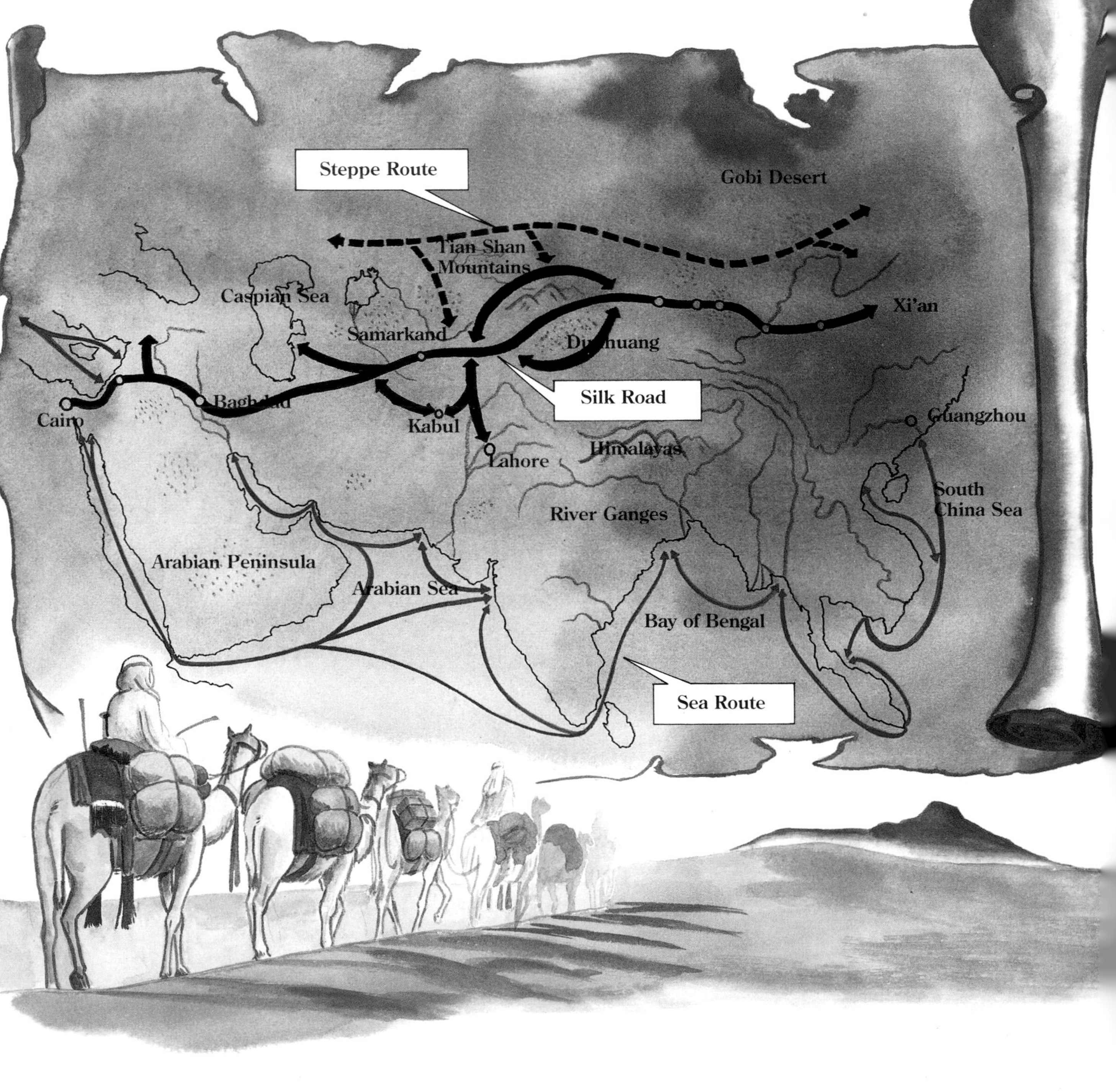

Steppe Route

Gobi Desert

Tian Shan Mountains

Caspian Sea

Samarkand

Dunhuang

Silk Road

Xi'an

Baghdad

Cairo

Kabul

Guangzhou

Lahore

Himalayas

South China Sea

Arabian Peninsula

River Ganges

Arabian Sea

Bay of Bengal

Sea Route

What Else Did They Use the Road For?

In addition to silk, many other products were carried along the road. There were carpets and precious stones, and things to eat such as fruits and vegetables. But travellers also took with them ideas and inventions. For instance, gunpowder and the way to make paper came to Europe along this road.

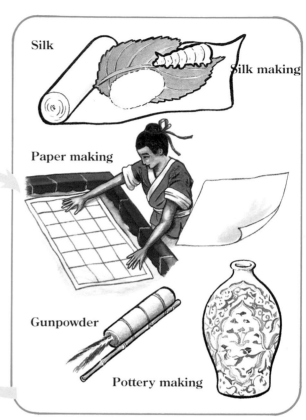

Silk

Silk making

Paper making

Gunpowder

Pottery making

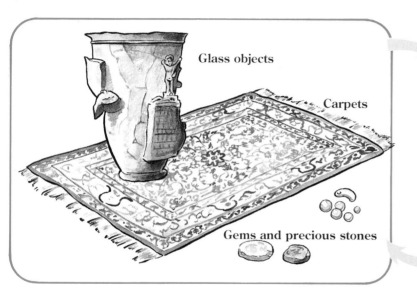

Glass objects

Carpets

Gems and precious stones

What Sort of Places Were There on the Road?

Much of the Silk Road followed trails through the desert. Along this route were places that had water, called oases, where people and their camels could rest. On the edge of one desert was the town of Dunhuang. It was one of the most important stops in and out of China. People from all over the world came through there. The town became a place where their ideas and cultures mixed together. As a result, many works of art and splendidly decorated houses from those earlier times can be seen in Dunhuang today.

● **To the Parent**

Portions of the Silk Road date back to about 2,000 B.C. Its route has changed with events. In the sixth century A.D., for example, Mesopotamia was the scene of bitter fighting between the Byzantine Empire and the Sassanid rulers of Persia. To avoid the area, caravans began taking a more northerly route so that the older, more central, Silk Road fell into disuse and oases along the way lost business.

▲ These houses are carved into the hillside. They are decorated with paintings that are very old.

How Were the Himalayas Formed?

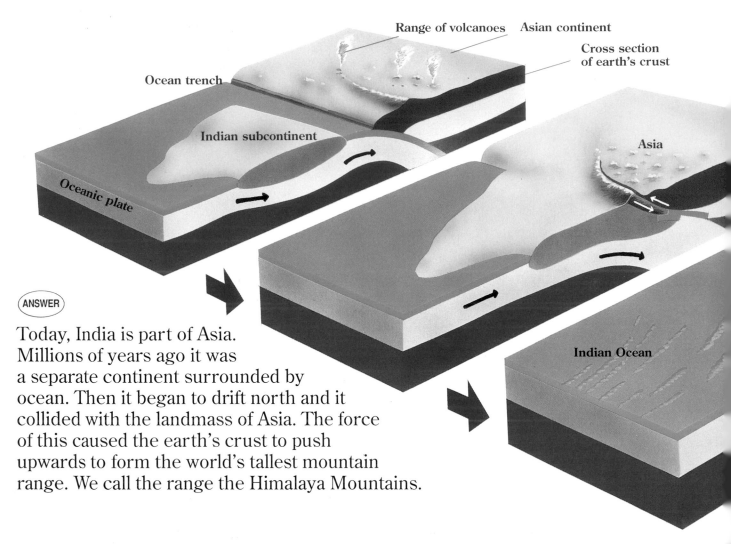

Range of volcanoes   Asian continent

Cross section of earth's crust

Ocean trench

Indian subcontinent

Oceanic plate

Asia

Indian Ocean

ANSWER

Today, India is part of Asia. Millions of years ago it was a separate continent surrounded by ocean. Then it began to drift north and it collided with the landmass of Asia. The force of this caused the earth's crust to push upwards to form the world's tallest mountain range. We call the range the Himalaya Mountains.

Roof of the World

The Himalayas are the highest mountain range in the world. This huge chain has 26 peaks that are 7,620 or more metres high. British-led climbers were the first to conquer the massive Mount Everest in 1953.

■ Fossil evidence

Shellfish live in the ocean. And yet fossils of shellfish have been found near the summit of Mount Everest, the world's highest peak. This proves that this mighty mountain was pushed up from the ocean floor.

▼ Many of the world's highest peaks are here.

Metres

9,000

6,000

3,000

Mt. Everest, Himalayas

K2, Karakoram Range

Mt. Aconcagua, Andes

Mt. McKinley, Alaska Range

Mt. Kilimanjaro, Tanzania

Mont Blanc, Alps

Matterhorn, Alps

Mt. Fuji, Japan

● To the Parent

The Himalayas were pushed up when India collided with the Asian landmass many millions of years ago. Where it squeezed below the landmass, there was a wrinkling of the earth's surface, and this is how the world's highest mountain range was formed. It is thought-provoking to reflect that these peaks once formed part of the ocean floor. It provides a concept of the passage of time and the incredible changes that have taken place on earth over millions of years.

Why Was the Taj Mahal Built?

ANSWER

The Taj Mahal was built by Shah Jahan, an emperor of India, in memory of his beloved wife, Mumtaz Mahal. Saddened by her death in 1631 he followed her last wish: she asked that he build a beautiful tomb in her memory so that her name would not be forgotten. Today, the Taj Mahal is one of the most famous buildings in the world, and Mumtaz Mahal is remembered as the queen who inspired it.

▼ **The Taj Mahal at Agra, India**

■ Matching views

The Taj Mahal was designed so that it looks the same viewed from any direction. The peaked dome is very large seen from the outside but it is even more impressive when seen from inside. It is hollow and rises to a height of nearly 30 metres above the surrounding structures.

▼ **Front view**

Hollow space

Coffin of Mumtaz Mahal

Coffin of Shah Jahan

▼ **Overhead view**

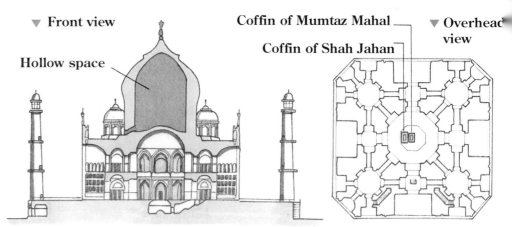

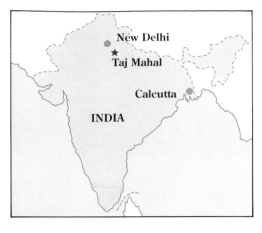

4 ...she contracts a fever and dies. She was only 36 years old.

1 Young Shah Jahan meets Mumtaz in the bazaar and falls in love.

5 It is said that Shah Jahan was so saddened by his wife's death that his hair turned white overnight.

2 They marry five years later. He is 20 years old, and she is just 17.

6 In memory of his beloved queen he builds the exquisite Taj Mahal.

3 Mumtaz bears many children, but after the 14th is born . . .

● **To the Parent**

Shah Jahan was the fifth ruler of the Mogul Empire. While Taj Mahal is a corruption of his wife's name and the monument is dedicated to her memory, it is believed that he also intended for it to stand as a spiritual focus of the Muslim faith in his empire. Craftsmen from as far away as Persia and the Middle East helped build it. Twenty thousand people worked on the building, which took 22 years to build. Today, the beautiful edifice of white marble is considered the perfect example of Mogul architecture, and many also believe it to be the most beautiful building in the world. It endures as a tribute to love and perfection.

❓ How Long Is the Great Wall?

ANSWER The Great Wall stretches from east to west across China. The distance from one end to the other is 2,400 kilometres, but the real length of the wall, as it snakes up and down hills and around obstructions, is nearly twice that great. It is said to be the only man-made structure that can be seen from the moon.

▶ China's Great Wall can be seen from the moon.

How Long Would It Take to Walk the Great Wall?

Visitors who come to China love to walk along the Great Wall. But imagine how long it would take to go from one end to the other. Suppose you walked 40 kilometres every single day. About how long do you think it would take you?

2,400 kilometres

The ends of the Great Wall are 2,400 kilometres apart. But you would have to walk about 4,800 kilometres as the wall twists and turns across China. Your walk would take four months to complete!

How Did They Build Such a Big Wall?

The Great Wall was built over many years by many thousands of workers.

1 Two huge fences were first built of logs, and then the space in between them was filled in to form the wall.

2 The original wall was built up with layers of packed earth, trees and reeds, and these were left to harden.

3 Later, the wall was restored. The outer sides were buttressed with bricks and stone, which have survived till now.

? Why Was the Wall Built?

The Great Wall of China was built to keep out wandering tribes that invaded China from time to time. The wall was begun in about the fifth century B.C. but fell into disrepair. In 221 B.C., the Emperor Shi Huang Di had it restored and completed. The wall is built of earth, brick and stone, and its height varies from six to nine metres. Tall watchtowers provide a view of the countryside.

● To the Parent

In 221 B.C., Emperor Shi Huang Di unified China for the first time under the Qin Dynasty. He ordered the reconstruction of the Great Wall to keep out invading nomads. The wall was maintained, more or less, by subsequent generations of emperors, but in the second half of the 16th century it was renovated in the form visible today.

？ Why Are These Hills So Famous?

(ANSWER) This beautiful scenery can be seen around the Chinese city of Guilin. The hills rise sharply out of the surrounding flat plains. The tallest hills reach 300 metres into the sky. They are famous because they are often seen in the paintings of Chinese artists. The odd shape of the hills is due to erosion. It took thousands of years for the hills to form.

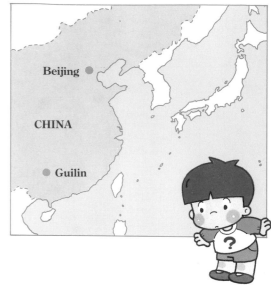

▼ The landscape of Guilin is often seen in Chinese paintings.

68

How Did the Hills Get Such Unusual Shapes?

Long ago, the land was covered with gently rolling hills. But the plains were made of a rock called limestone which dissolves in rainwater. When rain fell on the plains the rock began to dissolve. As plants grew, their roots broke up the ground and the rainwater seeped in. So the erosion continued below the surface and underground caverns formed.

1

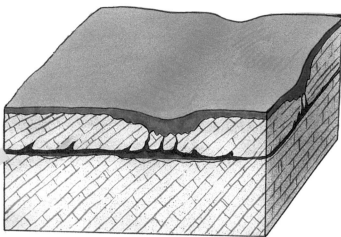

Above ground, the crevices in the limestone grew wider and deeper as more and more limestone was worn away. Eventually the parts that hadn't eroded were separated by huge gullies. As the water level fell the underground caverns dried out.

2

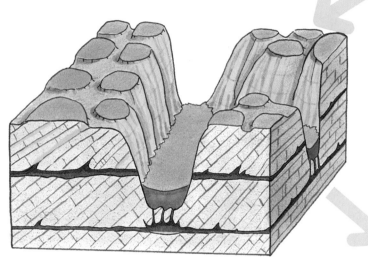

This erosion continued over many thousands of years, and the shape of the peaks became steeper and steeper. Beneath many of the hills of Guilin you can find the hollowed-out caverns that helped to form them.

3

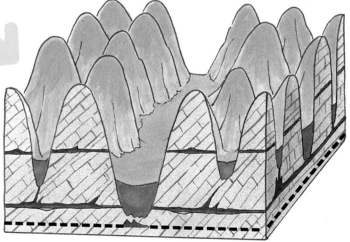

■ Stalactite caves

Stalactite caves are often found in limestone areas. Stalactites are formed when rainwater seeps through limestone, dissolving some of the lime. Water drips off the ceilings of underground caverns and some of it evaporates, leaving lime deposits which hang from the roof like icicles. These are called stalactites.

▲ **Stalactite cave at Guilin**

● **To the Parent**

Guilin's peaks are a favourite theme in the paintings of the southern school of Chinese art. Often the mist-shrouded mountains are depicted towering behind a lake or river upon which floats a sampan or a boat. The effect is quite enchanting, and many people assume that it is a figment of the artist's imagination. But such scenery actually exists in the Guilin region. The unusual landscape here results from the effect of an extremely hot, humid climate on the limestone bedrock. Pillars of limestone rising almost straight upwards, in the way that those at Guilin do, are found only in areas that are tropical or subtropical.

69

? **What Is the Longest Undersea Tunnel in the World?**

ANSWER The longest is the Seikan Tunnel, which runs between the Japanese islands of Honshu and Hokkaido. It is a 53-kilometre-long tunnel for trains. There is a railway platform inside the tunnel so passengers can get off the train and look around.

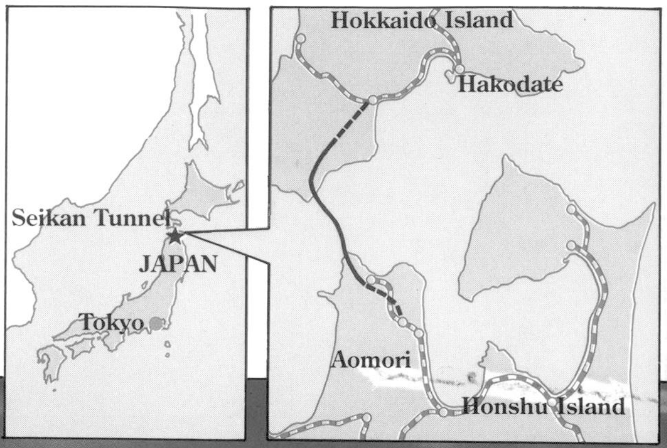

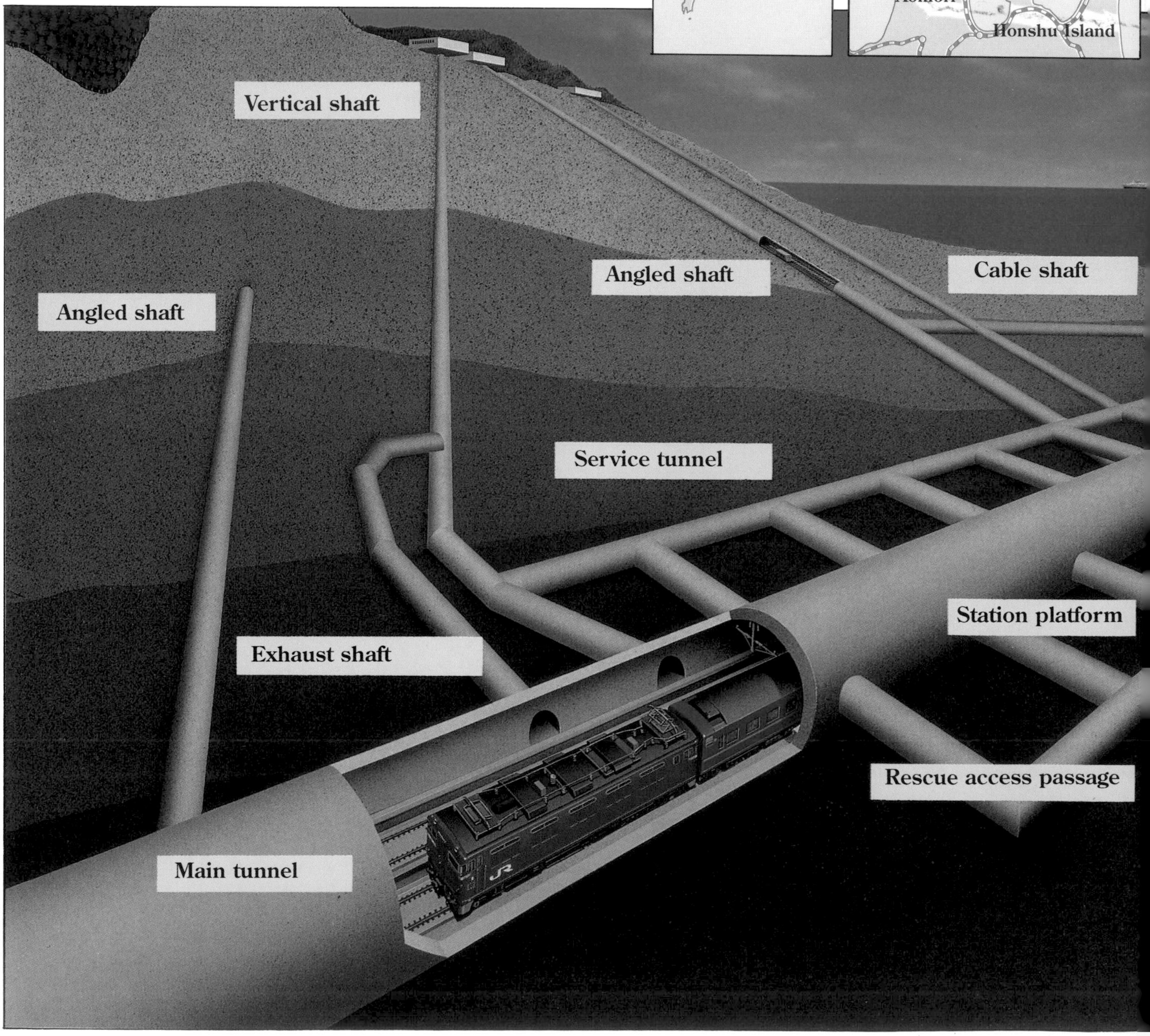

Hokkaido Island

Hakodate

Seikan Tunnel

JAPAN

Tokyo

Aomori

Honshu Island

Vertical shaft

Angled shaft

Cable shaft

Angled shaft

Service tunnel

Exhaust shaft

Station platform

Rescue access passage

Main tunnel

■ A cross section

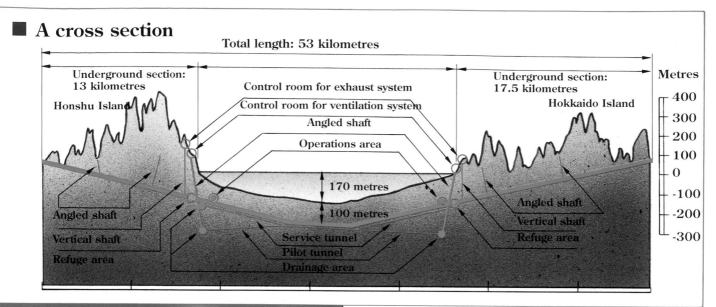

Total length: 53 kilometres

Underground section: 13 kilometres

Honshu Island

Control room for exhaust system
Control room for ventilation system
Angled shaft
Operations area

Underground section: 17.5 kilometres

Hokkaido Island

170 metres

100 metres

Angled shaft
Vertical shaft
Refuge area

Angled shaft
Vertical shaft
Refuge area

Service tunnel
Pilot tunnel
Drainage area

Metres
- 400
- 300
- 200
- 100
- 0
- -100
- -200
- -300

Fire tunnel

Pilot tunnel

▲ There is a passenger platform in the tunnel.

■ Some of the tunnel's measurements

The Seikan Tunnel is large. It is about eight metres high and nearly 10 metres across. The seamless railway track used in the tunnel is 52.5 kilometres long. The tunnel is fitted with the very best safety and rescue equipment.

▼ Equipment

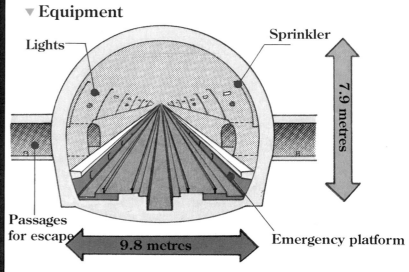

Lights

Sprinkler

7.9 metres

Passages for escape

9.8 metres

Emergency platform

● To the Parent

Starting with geological surveys in 1946, construction of the Seikan Tunnel took 42 years. Counting all the service and emergency escape tunnels there is a total of 18 tunnels with a length of nearly 72 kilometres. The railway track through the tunnel is the longest seamless track in the world. A station platform beneath the sea is the only such station to be found anywhere. The most up-to-date safety and rescue equipment, including laser measuring devices, was installed in the tunnel.

❓ Did You Know That the Largest Rock in the World Is in Australia?

(ANSWER) Ayers Rock is a single huge rock that rises out of a desert area in the centre of the Australian continent. It is the largest single rock anywhere in the world. It is a strange sort of hill, carved by nature from hard red sandstone that changes colour with the light.

▼ **Ayers Rock**

■ How high is this rock?

Ayers Rock reaches a height of about 350 metres above ground — higher than the Eiffel Tower in Paris! The Rock is over three kilometres long and the distance all the way round is nine kilometres. It looks very bare from far away, but there are places hidden from view with water, plants and animals.

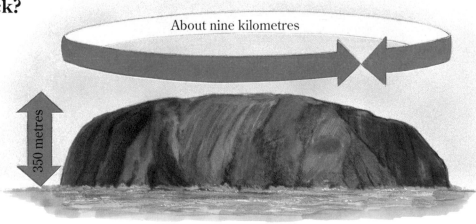

About nine kilometres

350 metres

How Was Such a Rock Formed?

In the centre of Australia, there is hardly any rainfall and the air currents are unusual. For more than 600 million years the dry winds eroded the rocky land, wearing it down and turning it into a desert. However, some rock was harder than the rest and did not get worn down, and this is how — some scientists think — this huge, loaf-shaped rock was left standing at almost the exact centre of Australia.

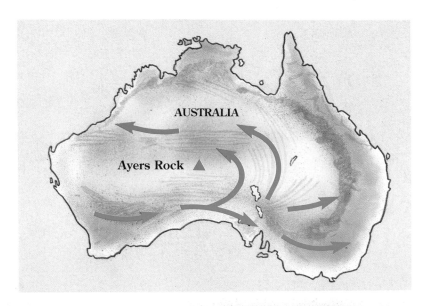

Air currents. The winds ▷ of the region seem to circle around Ayers Rock.

Before erosion began long ago this region was a flat plain.

Wind erosion gets under way, but one part of the area is unchanged.

Erosion continues and eventually forms what we now call Ayers Rock.

Does Australia Have Other Odd Land Formations?

Yes, it does. Wind and rain carved many strange rock shapes in this region of Australia. Their names describe what they look like — for example, Devil's Marbles, Kangaroo Tail, Organ Pipes and Wave Rock.

▽ **Devil's Marbles**

Wave Rock ▷

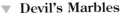

● **To the Parent**

Although Ayers Rock, now usually called by its aboriginal name *Uluru*, is surrounded by a dry featureless plain and the outer rock-face is bare, wind and rain have eroded the upper rock into many parallel gullies. In these, rainwater collects and both vegetation and animals thrive. Ayers Rock and the area around it, including Mount Olga, 32 kilometres to the west, are now a National Park. Since the first rocks were formed billions of years ago the landscape of this isolated continent has undergone few major changes.

What Makes the Great Barrier Reef So Famous?

ANSWER The Great Barrier Reef is the largest coral reef in the world. It stretches for about 2,000 kilometres along the coast of Australia. It is made from the skeletons of billions of tiny creatures called coral. These creatures live in colonies that are hundreds of years old.

▲ The reef is an actual coastal barrier.

How the Great Barrier Reef Was Formed

The temperature of the ocean must be between 20° and 30°C with adequate sunlight for coral to survive. So the coral live close to the surface.

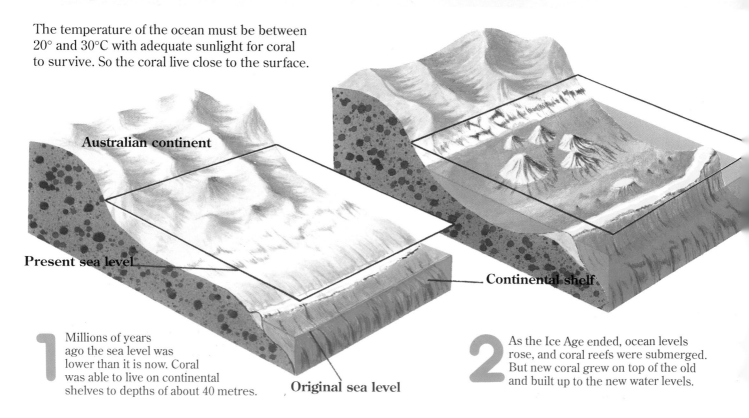

1 Millions of years ago the sea level was lower than it is now. Coral was able to live on continental shelves to depths of about 40 metres.

Present sea level

Original sea level

2 As the Ice Age ended, ocean levels rose, and coral reefs were submerged. But new coral grew on top of the old and built up to the new water levels.

Continental shelf

Australian continent

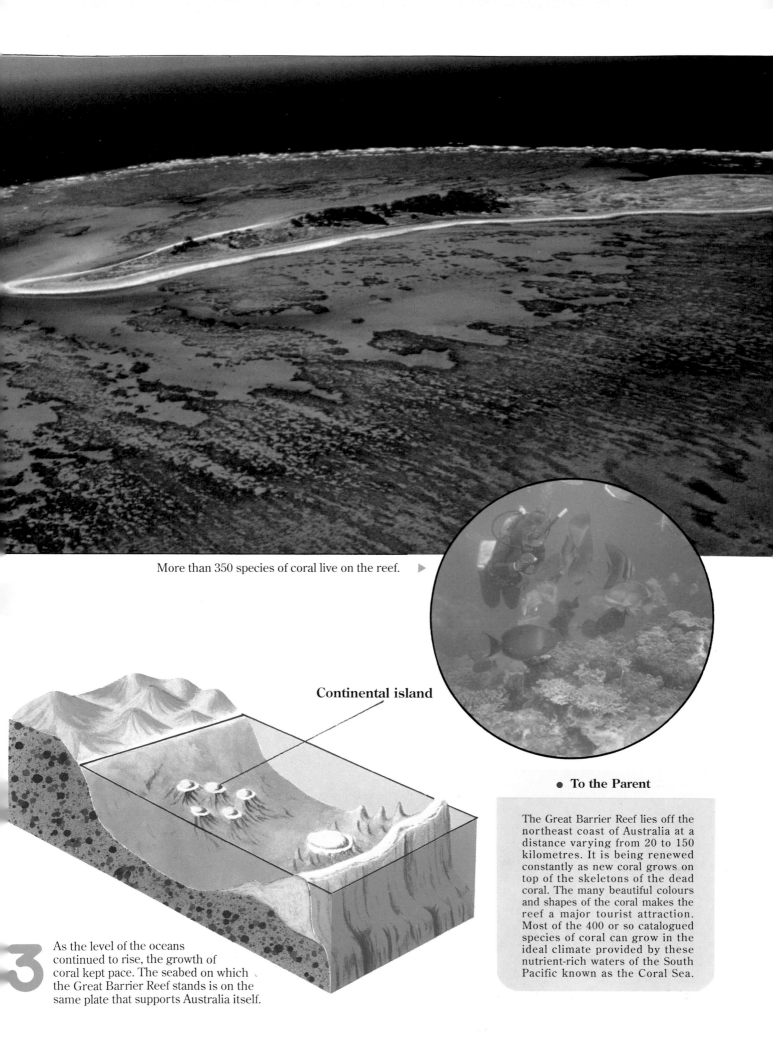

More than 350 species of coral live on the reef. ▶

Continental island

As the level of the oceans
continued to rise, the growth of
coral kept pace. The seabed on which
the Great Barrier Reef stands is on the
same plate that supports Australia itself.

● **To the Parent**

The Great Barrier Reef lies off the
northeast coast of Australia at a
distance varying from 20 to 150
kilometres. It is being renewed
constantly as new coral grows on
top of the skeletons of the dead
coral. The many beautiful colours
and shapes of the coral makes the
reef a major tourist attraction.
Most of the 400 or so catalogued
species of coral can grow in the
ideal climate provided by these
nutrient-rich waters of the South
Pacific known as the Coral Sea.

What Kind of Place Is Antarctica?

(ANSWER) Antarctica is the land of the South Pole. It is one of the continents, only slightly smaller than South America. It is the coldest place on earth. Even in summer the temperature never goes above -29°C. Many nations have research bases there, but Antarctica is not owned by any one nation.

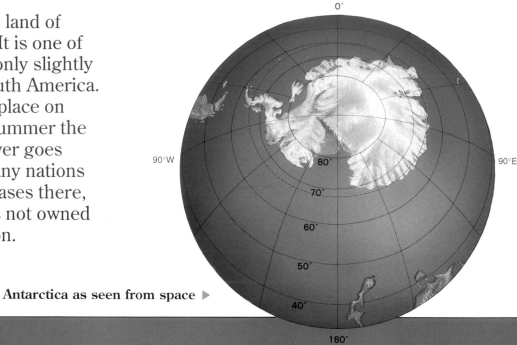

Antarctica as seen from space ▶

▲ Penguins are the best-known inhabitants of Antarctica. Most species of penguin live only in Antarctica.

How thick is the ice there?

Almost all of Antarctica is covered by a thick cap of ice.
Its average thickness is just under two kilometres.

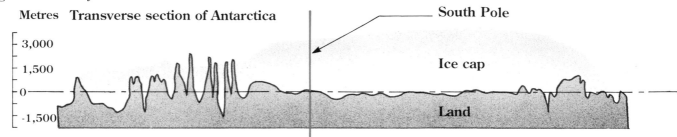

Metres **Transverse section of Antarctica**

South Pole

Ice cap

Land

3,000
1,500
0
-1,500

Days without nights

In December and January, the
sun never sets in the Antarctic.
This photograph shows how the
sun moves but does not set.
There are 24 hours of daylight.

Aurora

The aurora is a beautiful
light visible at the North
and South Poles. Over
Antarctica the aurora
is sometimes known as
the Southern Lights.

The animals of Antarctica

Penguins, seals and seagulls are some of
the natural inhabitants of the continent.

◀ **Seals**   ▲ **Penguins**

● **To the Parent**

In contrast to the Arctic, which
is merely a huge pack of ice with
no land beneath it, Antarctica is
an enormous ice-covered continent.
The presence of this continent was
confirmed in 1820. After that a
race developed between explorers
from many nations to reach the
South Pole. A team from Norway,
led by Roald Amundsen, was the
first to succeed when it arrived
at the pole on December 14, 1911.

❓ What Are These?

■ Cologne Cathedral

This is a picture of Cologne Cathedral in West Germany. It is one of the most famous churches in Europe. People began working on it in the year 1248. Work continued on and off for centuries. It took over 600 years to completely build it! Its twin spires are 157 metres tall. The building is 143 metres long by 53 metres wide. Cologne Cathedral was badly damaged during World War II. After the war, it was carefully repaired.

■ Westminster Abbey

This is Westminster Abbey in London, one of the most famous places in England. It is where the kings and queens of England have been crowned since William the Conqueror. A church has stood on this site for more than 1,000 years, but the main abbey seen today is only about 700 years old. Many famous architects helped to design the abbey over the years, and many of England's most famous people are buried here.

■ Fontainebleau Palace

Fontainebleau sits in its own beautiful gardens surrounded by forest. It was once a hunting lodge used by the kings of France. But in about 1527, French and Italian craftsmen turned it into a large, elegant palace. It is about 65 kilometres from Paris and is now a public museum.

■ Schönbrunn Palace

This magnificent palace is in Vienna, the capital city of Austria. It is just how most people imagine a palace to be. There are over 1,400 rooms in the palace and it is surrounded by beautiful gardens and trees. Schönbrunn was one of the homes of the royal Hapsburg family that once ruled Austria.

■ The Matterhorn

The Matterhorn is a mountain on the border between Switzerland and Italy. It is easily recognized because of its majestic shape. Although not nearly as high as some other mountains (it is 4,477 metres high), the Matterhorn's very steep peak presents a great challenge to mountain climbers.

■ The White House

The White House in Washington, D.C., is the home of the President of the United States. It was burned by British soldiers during the War of 1812, and when rebuilt it was painted white — one reason for its name. There are about 130 rooms. The President and his family live on the second floor.

● **To the Parent**

There are impressive buildings, beautiful landscapes and places of special historical importance in every corner of the globe. Stories about them are often fascinating and contribute to the visitors' enjoyment. Such stories will also make learning about them more enjoyable for your child and provide a greater awareness of other lands.

? And These?

■ Temples of Abu Simbel

The Temples of Abu Simbel were built by the ancient Egyptians more than 3,000 years ago. They were carved out of stone on the bank of the River Nile. When the Aswan High Dam was built, it was feared that water would destroy the temples. To save them, they were moved to a new location.

■ Sydney Opera House

The Sydney Opera House has become Australia's most famous building. Its unusual design makes it immediately recognizable. The building took 16 years to construct, cost $102 million and was opened by Queen Elizabeth II in 1973. There are four performance halls.

■ Temple of the Emerald Buddha

This beautiful temple is in Bangkok, Thailand. The people there call it Wat Phra Keo. Inside is a statue of Buddha, who is special to the religion of the Thai people. Some of the clothes that this Buddha wears are made of real gold.

● **To the Parent**

Our world contains many wonderful things. Different countries of the world have unique features and sights that cannot be found in the reader's own country. Teaching your children about such places is an easy way to help them learn about other peoples' daily lives and customs.

Growing-Up Album

Where Are These Famous Places?

Can you name the countries where you will find the places shown in the photographs on these pages? Look at the map of the world and try to spot them. If you don't know, don't be afraid to guess.

3 **Stonehenge.** No one knows for sure who put these gigantic stones here or what their meaning is.

1 **Statue of Liberty.** This statue is said to symbolize the freedom that the citizens of this country enjoy. It stands in a famous harbour.

2 **Mount Rushmore.** The faces of four outstanding former presidents of this country are carved out of the cliff face. A father and son carved them.

4 **Leaning Tower.** This famous tower has tilted like this almost since it was built hundreds of years ago.

The Kremlin. Located in the capital of the nation, it is important in the country's political and cultural life.

The Great Wall. It is 2,400 kilometres long and was built many centuries ago to keep out troublesome invaders.

7 Taj Mahal. It is one of the world's most beautiful buildings. A king ordered it to be built as a memorial to his dead queen.

Answers:

1 United States	5 U.S.S.R.
2 United States	6 People's Republic of China
3 Great Britain	7 India
4 Italy	

Have You Ever Seen These Before?

Look at the illustrations on these pages. If you have ever been to any of these countries and seen these things for yourself put a tick by them. If you have read about them in another book or seen them on television put a double tick. If you have read about them in this book put three ticks.

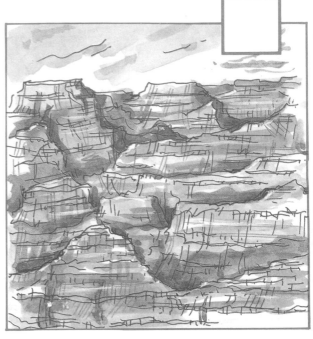

Grand Canyon. This enormous deep gorge was cut by the Colorado River. It is in Arizona.

Windmills in Holland. Windmills were used in the past to pump water and to mill grain by harnessing the power of the wind. They provided free energy.

The Pyramids. Built long ago, using huge stone blocks long, they were the tombs of Egypt's pharaohs.

Niagara Falls. This most famous waterfall of all is on the border between the United States and Canada.

Eiffel Tower. This is the world-famous landmark of Paris. Over 300 metres high, it dominates the skyline.

Ayers Rock. Located almost in the centre of Australia, it is the single biggest rock found in the world. It is almost flat on top.

The Colosseum. Men fought for their lives in this arena in Rome.

Tower Bridge. It spans the River Thames and is one of London's best-known landmarks.

The Parthenon. This is what remains of a great temple in Athens, dedicated to a goddess of ancient Greece.

Match the Words and Pictures

Look at the descriptions of famous places numbered 1 to 8 and match them to the correct illustration. Write the correct number in the space provided beside the description.

1 Vatican City

2 Sahara

3 Venice

4 Antarctica

These are long, deep inlets formed by glaciers thousands of years ago along the coasts of Northern Europe.	

This is a shortcut between the Atlantic and Pacific oceans for ships. It is in Central America.	

The longest undersea tunnel in the world, it connects two islands of Japan. It took 42 years to build.	

The smallest country in the world, it is surrounded by the city of Rome. It has many famous paintings.	

5 Easter Island

7 Seikan Tunnel

6 Panama Canal

8 Scandinavian fjord

This Italian city is famous for its many canals and its gondolas. Once it was an important trading centre.

This place is famous for its many huge stone statues. No one is sure how or why they happen to be there.

This huge region in Africa is covered entirely by sand. Rain seldom falls, and not many animals can survive here.

This is the southernmost part of the world. It is covered with snow and ice. Many penguins live there.

A Child's First Library of Learning

Famous Places

ISBN 0 7054 1046 3
TIME-LIFE is a trademark of
Time Warner Inc. U.S.A.

Photos:
Pacific Press Service; Orion Press; Bon Color;
Australia Travel Bureau; Tourism Australia.

Editorial Supervision by:
International Editorial Services Inc.
Tokyo, Japan

Editor: C. E. Berry
Associate Editor: Winston S. Priest
Writer: James H. Shaw
Translation: Pauline Bush
Editorial Assistant: Nobuko Abe

EUROPEAN EDITION:
Gillian Moore, Ed Skyner, Ilse Gray, Wendy Gibbons
Editorial Production:
Maureen Kelly, Samantha Hill,
Theresa John, Debra Lelliott

Editorial Consultant for the Series: Andrew Gutelle

Typesetting by G. Beard & Son Ltd, Brighton, Sussex, England.
Printed by GEA, Milan, and bound by GEP, Cremona, Italy.

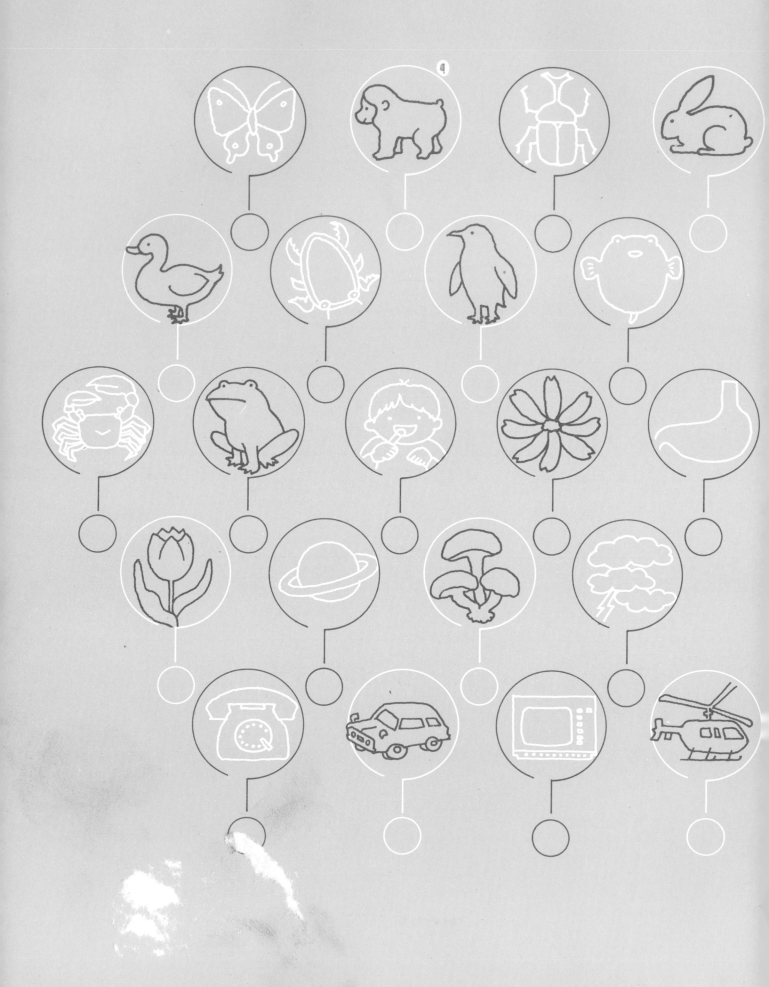